D. M. HUTCHINSON

Lamb
Around
the World

Lamb Around the World

ORIGINALLY PUBLISHED UNDER THE TITLE

Lamb Favorites Old & New

RANDOM HOUSE ∗ *New York*

Book design by Mary M. Ahern

9 8 7 6 5 4 3 2

FIRST PAPERBACK EDITION

Contents

✻✻✻✻✻✻✻✻✻ ✻✻✻✻✻✻✻✻ ✻✻✻✻✻✻

Lamb
Around
the World

You've Never Cooked Lamb?

No matter. It's not too late to start right now. There's nothing mysterious about lamb cookery. Treat this distinctive meat as you would any red meat, bearing in mind that low temperatures are best for roasting all meat.

In this volume you will find recipes for all cuts of lamb ranging from simple everyday types to gourmet dishes with an international flavor for those special occasions when you want to serve something really outstanding. I hope that by including a wide variety of recipes, along with basic cookery suggestions, every homemaker will find recipes in this book that she will use and make her own. Both domestic and foreign recipes are arranged by cut. See detailed information about each cut at the beginning of each section.

Happy cooking!

Some Questions Answered

❧❧❧❧❧❧❧❧❧ ❧❧❧❧❧❧❧❧❧ ❧❧❧❧❧

When is lamb available?

The heaviest supply of lamb usually comes to market in the fall, but thanks to the geographically widespread nature of the lamb business and the varying weather conditions from section to section, lamb is now available every month of the year. It is no longer considered a seasonal meat, as it once was. The supply of fresh American lamb has now been augmented by supplies of frozen New Zealand and Australian lamb in many parts of the country. All such imported lamb must pass United States inspection.

Is genuine lamb always small?

Lamb to be sold in this country as lamb has to be less than twelve months of age. Size has little to do with it. Because of improved breeding and feeding methods, many lambs come to market weighing around 60 pounds dressed, which is larger than in past years. This meatier lamb supplies a better ratio of meat to bone and can be both lean and succulent. Since lambs marketed in this country usually average about six months of age (some may be even younger) and can never be over twelve months old, you will find that lamb is always tender.

Sometimes in January, February, and March, in certain sections of this country, one sees "hothouse" lambs weighing from 17 to 25 pounds. These are usually from six to eight weeks old and are much in demand by certain ethnic groups who like to roast them whole.

Occasionally you will see "yearlings" advertised. These are a year old or older, but less than two years. Ninety-four percent of all ovines slaughtered in this country are lambs. Practically no true mutton is available on the retail market, since most of it goes to commercial processors or to certain gourmet restaurants where mutton is a feature on the menu.

How do you know what you're buying?

The answer to the above question is, "Know your meat resource." Meat merchandisers know that lamb carcasses have "break joints" in the foreshanks and that they have narrow rib bones. The meat is fine-textured. Forequarters are usually narrow and compact. When the forefeet are broken off at the break joint, a series of well-defined points will be exposed. With advancing age, these become rounded and decrease in number. Since, as a consumer, you will probably never see this, it is important to deal with a reputable meat merchandiser.

High-quality lamb has a smooth covering of clear pinkish-white brittle fat over most of the exterior. Over this is a thin paper-like covering called the fell. The fell is usually removed from chops. Ordinarily it should not be removed from legs, however, as it will help the leg to hold its shape better and to be more juicy.

Is all lamb tender?

Usually all cuts of lamb are tender since the meat comes from young animals less than a year old. This means it is possible to cook all cuts by the dry-heat method of cooking if the cooking is handled carefully. Some cuts, in the author's opinion, however, are better braised. These are the shoulder chops, neck slices, shanks and the breast. Legs, loins and racks may be roasted. Steaks and loin and rib chops may be broiled, pan-broiled or fried, according to taste.

Regardless of cut or cookery method, low cooking temperatures are best if tenderness is to be preserved. Cook according to cut. Avoid overcooking.

What about care and storage of fresh lamb?

If fresh lamb is brought home from a self-service market and is to be used within a day or two, it need not be removed from its film wrappings. It should be stored in the coldest part of the refrigerator, however, at a temperature of from 32° to 40° F. If meat is to be stored more than two days, remove wrappings and cover loosely with wax paper. It is unwise to try to keep fresh meat in the average refrigerator any longer than absolutely necessary. If it is not to be used by the end of the fourth day, it is best to freeze it.

Ground lamb should not be held unfrozen more than twenty-four hours, since no ground meat has the keeping qualities of solid pieces. Variety meats, such as liver, kidney, and heart, do not keep as well as muscle meats and should be used as soon after purchasing as possible, or should be frozen or precooked.

Fresh-frozen lamb

When you buy frozen lamb, leave it in its moisture-vapor proof wrapping, and transfer it immediately to your home freezer for storage at zero degrees or colder, unless you plan to cook it promptly. Lamb, like poultry and other meats, may be cooked from the frozen state, or thawed. To thaw, loosen wrap and let stand in the refrigerator or on a kitchen counter. Once the meat has been thawed, use it at once, do not refreeze.

To freeze fresh lamb, package it in moisture-vapor proof freezer wrap in convenient amounts for later cooking and serving. Separate individual chops and patties with freezer paper. Wrap as snugly as possible, and close with a double fold, to seal out the air, then label with the amount, cut and date, and place in the coldest part of the freezer.

Is refrigerator space limited?

It is wise once a meal is over to remove meat from bones such as the bone in a leg of lamb or the bone in a square-cut shoulder of lamb to save storage space. The meat will then be easier to cover to prevent drying.

How do I prepare the less familiar cuts?

Most familiar cuts of lamb are very lean, with little marbling and with outside fat that can be removed very easily. In the case of cuts such as riblets, however, it is suggested that any excess fat be trimmed away before cooking and that, after browning, the drippings be poured off before adding any kind of sauce. Barbecued riblets are particularly delicious when this practice is observed. Some people also like to simmer the less expensive cuts (which often contain more fat) until done, then cool overnight so fat can be lifted from the top in one congealed sheet the following morning. Remembering to dispose of excess fat will make many inexpensive dishes more popular and will enable the homemaker to save money on her budget.

What are the basic cookery methods?

There are two basic cookery methods for lamb:
(1) *Dry Heat* This method includes roasting, broiling, pan-broiling, pan-frying, griddle-frying and in special cases (as for croquettes) deep-fat frying.
(2) *Moist Heat* Moist heat cookery includes braising and cooking in liquid.

What is the best temperature to use for roasting?

A low temperature of no more than 325° F. is recommended for roasting. This low temperature holds shrinkage and loss of juices to a minimum, makes for even cooking and browning and more appealing flavor.

Use of an internal meat thermometer is also recommended in roasting. Place the thermometer in the thickest part of the meat, making sure it does not rest against bone or in a pocket of fat. Degree of doneness is a highly personal thing. We suggest the following guide:

Rare	140°–150°F.
Medium	160°–165°F.
Well done	170°–180°F.

Should I sear a roast?

Searing has long been advocated by French chefs. While it produces an excellent roast if properly done, it is a wasteful cookery method resulting in more shrink, more oven spattering and sometimes smoke and excessive cooking odors. If you feel you still want to try a seared roast, start roasting at 425°-450°F. for 15 to 20 minutes to brown, then reduce heat to 325°F. and continue roasting to desired degree of internal doneness.

In sautéeing ground or cubed lamb, should shortening be used?

Normally it is not necessary to use fat in browning ground or cubed lamb since sufficient natural fat is present in the meat. In the event that the lamb is extremely lean, as it may be sometimes, use a tablespoonful or two of shortening for browning. Drain off any surplus fat after browning before proceeding with the recipe.

In the recipes calling for ground or cubed lamb, a minimum of 1 tablespoon of shortening has been used. The amount of shortening indicated for browning may be adjusted to slightly more if necessary.

Basting?

Basting is necessary only when roasting on a spit or when a glaze or flavor-adding sauce is used. It is not necessary in oven-roasting. Place the roast on a rack in a pan, fat-side up. As the meat cooks, the melting fat will run over and into the meat. This self-basting is sufficient. If gravy is desired, part of the fat drippings under the rack can be reserved for making the desired amount of gravy.

Should a roast be covered?

Meat should not be covered if a true roast is desired. When the roaster cover is used, the end product will in reality be cooked partially by the moisture which escapes from the meat, and the end result, though tasty, will not be a true roast. This is not to indicate that the old-fashioned way of preparing roast cuts should never be used if one enjoys meat prepared this way, but only to point out that meat prepared in a covered roaster will in effect be braised rather than roasted, and the taste will not be the same.

What serving temperature is best?

Lamb is considered to have the best flavor when it is served very hot on hot plates or thoroughly chilled.

When should I salt?

In the case of roasts, stews and braised dishes, salt may be added at the beginning of the cooking period. In broiling, however, it is best to brown the top side of the meat thoroughly before adding salt because salt has a tendency to draw juices up out of the meat and make it drier. After browning the top, salt the meat, turn it, brown the bottom side, and salt again.

In broiling, pan-frying or grilling, it is best never to turn the meat more than once if you can help it.

Should I use tongs or a fork for turning chops and steaks?

Since piercing meat with a fork tends to release juices, tongs are best for turning. If a fork must be used, insert it if possible in the outer rim of fat.

What about glands?

The popliteal gland occurs just above the hock joint in a leg of lamb. This gland, sometimes called the musk gland, is mistakenly believed by some to cause an odor in cooking and a strong flavor. This is not true.

A similar gland, the prescapular, is found in the shoulder and is seldom, if ever, removed unless the shoulder is completely boned.

Both of these glands are in reality lymph glands. They are approximately as large in the small animals as in the larger ones and are therefore by comparison more conspicuous in small animals. These glands should cause the consumer no concern whatever. They have no effect either on odor or flavor. The identical glands are also found in beef and pork and are removed only if the surrounding fat makes the cut look undesirable.

The only thing that can cause an undesirable odor in cooking is the use of too high a temperature. Lamb fat is classed as "hard" fat and burns at a lower degree of heat than certain other animal fats.

What about rare lamb?

It is perfectly safe to serve lamb rare since lambs are clean, unusually healthy animals. A bit of experimenting on the cook's part will determine the degree of doneness liked best by her family. The majority of people seem to prefer an internal temperature of somewhere between 170° and 180° F. Some gourmets, on the other hand, sometimes like lamb as rare as 140° F. No matter what degree of doneness you like, allow a roast to stand in a warm place for about fifteen minutes after removal from the oven to give it a chance to firm up. This makes slicing much easier.

Nutrient Content

Lamb Cut	Cooked Weight Oz.	Measure as Consumed	Protein Gm.	Calories
Arm Chop	3½		25.7	252
Blade Chop	3½	4″ x 2″ x ¾″ TH	27.4	280
Loin Chop	3½		27.1	223
Rib Chop	3½		25.5	291
Roast Leg— Whole	3½	4″ x 3″ x ½″ TH	28.2	195
Roast Leg— Center Cut	3½		28.3	182
Riblets	3½		23.5	399

Courtesy National Live Stock & Meat Board

Based on Research of R. M. Leverton, Ph.D., and G. V. Odell, 1958
Nutrient Content of Cooked Meats 100 Gm.

Calcium Mg.	Phosphorus Mg.	Magnesium Mg.	Iron* Mg.	Thiamine Mg.	Riboflavin Mg.	Niacin Mg.
	236	24.5				
	243	23.4				
8.2	214	24.1	2.8	0.21	0.33	7.9
	220	20.4	2.8			
8.2	215	23.6	3.6	0.23	0.31	7.3
		23.3				
	158	19.5				

* Calculated Dr. Schweigert's Bulletin No. 30. Blank spaces indicate no analysis made.

"How To" Tips

HOW TO ROAST
Season with salt, pepper and herbs, if desired. Place fat-side up on rack in open roasting pan. Insert meat thermometer, making sure it does not rest in fat or against bone. Roast at 325° F. Add no water. Do not cover. Do not baste. Roast to degree of doneness desired.

HOW TO BROIL
Set oven regulator for broiling. Place meat on broiler rack two to three inches from heat. Broil until top of meat is brown, season with salt and pepper, turn and brown other side. Season and serve immediately.

HOW TO PAN-BROIL
Place meat in heavy frying pan. Cook over low heat without adding fat or water. Do not cover. Turn to insure even cooking, pouring off fat as it accumulates. Brown meat well on both sides but do not overcook. Season.

HOW TO PAN-FRY
Brown on both sides in a small amount of fat. Season meat. Do not cover. Cook at moderate temperature until done, turning occasionally. Serve at once.

HOW TO DEEP-FAT FRY
Coat meat with seasoned flour, cornmeal, crumbs, or batter. Fry a few servings at a time in enough fat to cover meat, using approximately 350° F. temperature for frying. Continue to cook until meat is done inside and is golden brown and crisp outside. Remove from frying kettle and drain; serve at once.

HOW TO BRAISE
Brown meat on all sides in fat in heavy utensil. Season. Add small amount of liquid. Cover tightly and cook at simmering temperature until tender.

HOW TO SIMMER LARGE CUTS
Cover meat with hot or cold water. Season with salt and pepper. Cover kettle tightly. Cook below boiling point until tender. Add vegetables, if desired, just long enough before serving to be cooked to required doneness.

HOW TO SIMMER STEWS
Cut meat in one- to two-inch pieces and brown on all sides in fat, if desired. Browning is not essential, however, if you prefer unbrowned stews. Season. Cover with water and cover kettle tightly. Cook slowly until tender. Add vegetables just long enough before serving to be cooked properly.

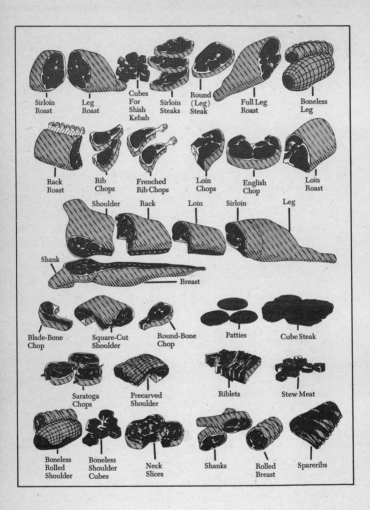

Sirloin Roast

Leg Roast

Cubes For Shish Kebab

Sirloin Steaks

Round (Leg) Steak

Full Leg Roast

Boneless Leg

Rack Roast

Rib Chops

Frenched Rib Chops

Loin Chops

English Chop

Loin Roast

Shoulder

Rack

Loin

Sirloin

Leg

Shank

Breast

Blade-Bone Chop

Square-Cut Shoulder

Round-Bone Chop

Patties

Cube Steak

Saratoga Chops

Precarved Shoulder

Riblets

Stew Meat

Boneless Rolled Shoulder

Boneless Shoulder Cubes

Neck Slices

Shanks

Rolled Breast

Spareribs

Identification of Cuts

Lamb is easy to cook, but there are three important rules
to follow:
  (1) cook according to the cut;
  (2) always use low temperature;
  (3) avoid overcooking.

Practically all lamb cuts are tender, so they can easily be
cooked by dry heat. Leg, shoulder, rib, and loin section are
usually roasted. Chops from these cuts are broiled, pan-
broiled, or fried. Shanks, breast, riblets, stew meat, and
neck slices should be cooked by moist heat by either braising
or simmering. Shoulder chops may also be braised.

Lamb is best served piping hot or well chilled.

NETTED BONELESS LEG
Contains meat from the whole leg, boned and held in solid slices by the addition of powdered egg white or wheat gluten which acts as a binder when leg is roasted. Roast fat-side up. After roasting, netting is slit on top side and peeled *down* to remove.
Roast in netting. Broil, grill filets.

NETTED BONELESS SHOULDER
Contains meat from whole shoulder, boned and held together with powdered egg white or wheat gluten as above. Should be handled same as netted leg.
Roast in netting. Broil, grill, braise filets.

NETTED SCOTCH ROAST
Same as roast described on p. 22 except for its elastic net cover. Treat as on p. 22.
Roast Scotch roast whole. Chops may be broiled or grilled.

SQUARE-CUT SHOULDER
Contains the arm, blade, rib bones and part of the neck bone. Blade bone exposed on rib side, arm bone on shank side. Layers of meat are interspersed with fat and outer surface covered by fat and fell (the thin skin or membrane covering the meat).
Roast.

PRECARVED SHOULDER
The square-cut shoulder is sliced through the bones on the band saw and tied firmly to be roasted whole. To serve, cords are snipped and removed. Slices are ready to serve.
Pot-roast, oven-braise, roast.

CUSHION SHOULDER
Made by removing the bones in the square-cut shoulder and sewing the pocket opening closed with twine. Sometimes filled with stuffing. Gets its name from the appearance of a cushion. Fell is not removed.
Roast.

COMBINATION SHOULDER
See round-bone and blade-bone chop description, also stew description which follows: Packaging the square-cut shoulder cut into two types of chops with remainder of shoulder cubed provides more than one convenient economical meal from the shoulder.
Broil, pan-broil, pan-fry, braise.
Simmer stew meat.

BONELESS ROLLED SHOULDER
After removing the bones in the square-cut shoulder, meat is rolled with the blade side exposed and tied with twine. Fat is distributed throughout the roast and covers outer surface of meat.
Roast or pot-roast.

ROUND-BONE SHOULDER CHOP
Round-bone shoulder chops are cut from the arm side of the square shoulder. These chops are usually free from excessive fat, the bone waste is slight, they are tasty and satisfying.
Broil, pan-broil, pan-fry, braise.

SHOULDER BLADE CHOPS
Blade chops contain blade bone, rib and backbone and the inside shoulder and clod muscles.
Broil, pan-broil, pan-fry, braise.

BONELESS STEW
May be cut from any part of the lamb carcass but usually from the forequarter cuts such as neck slices and shoulders. Lean, since nearly all fat is usually trimmed away.
Simmer in liquid.

SHISH KEBABS
Cubes of boneless lamb cut from the shoulder or leg and skewered may be found pre-threaded on wooden skewers in some markets or cubes may be sold in bulk.
Charcoal-broil, oven-broil.

SARATOGA CHOPS OR ROLL
Made from the inside shoulder muscle that is rolled and fastened with skewers and cut into chops. Little fat within the meat. No fat or fell covers outer surface.
Broil, pan-broil, pan-fry, braise.

LAMB NECK
Slices cut across neck exposing the neck muscles and the back strap (yellow connecting tissue) and the neckbone. Layers of meat interspersed with fat. Fat covers outside of slice.
Braise, simmer in liquid.

LAMB SHANKS
Front shanks of lamb containing the two foreshank bones, elbow and part of arm bone which is exposed on one surface. Layers of meat surround the bones and they are covered by fell. Because of their shape, they are sometimes called lamb drumsticks.
Braise, simmer in liquid.

CUBE STEAKS
Cube steaks are scored slices of lean brisket, and are a virtually fat-free, tender cut. Ideal for sandwiches.
Grill, braise, broil with moist topping.

LAMB BREAST

Contains the rib bones, breastbone and rib cartilages. Layers of fat and lean cover the bones on outer surface as well as inside over rib cartilages and breastbone. Flank end is boneless.

Braise, roast.

SCOTCH CHOPS AND ROAST

A Scotch roast is formed by slitting a pocket in a whole breast of lamb and stuffing with ground lamb or a mixture of ground lamb, bread crumbs or rice. Scotch chops are simply slices of Scotch roast cut between the rib bones.

Broil, grill, roast.

RIBLETS (BREAST)

Cuts made from the breast by cutting between rib bones. Alternating layers of fat and lean and cross sections of the rib cartilages are exposed on cut surface. Rib bones exposed at thin end of riblets.

Braise, simmer in liquid.

SPARERIBS AND PINWHEELS

Spareribs are made by trimming off all fat from breast section, exposing lean meaty portion. Pinwheels are formed by rolling and skewering the entire boneless defatted breast and slicing into slices approximately one inch thick.

Braise, barbecue.

GROUND LAMB

Boneless lamb from the neck, breast,
shanks, and flank is generally used in
making ground lamb, although any part
can be boned and ground.
Grill, roast, bake.

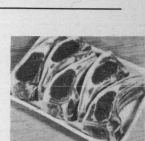

RIB CHOPS

Contains the backbone and, depending on
thickness, a rib bone. Meaty area is the
eye of the rib with fat and lean
surrounding it. Outer surface covered by
fat with the fell removed.
Broil, pan-broil, pan-fry.

RACK ROAST

Bones include the backbone and ribs,
the number of which is dependent
on size. The eye of the rib is covered
with fat. Thin ends of the ribs covered
with layers of fat and lean.
Roast.

FRENCH ROAST

Same as above except that fingers of meat
between rib bone ends have been
removed to a depth of approximately one
and one-half inches. After roasting, rib
ends may be covered with paper frills,
whole boiled onions, jumbo pitted olives,
small new potatoes, etc.
Roast.

CROWN ROAST

Made with at least two rib roasts (rack) with the backbone removed, shaped into a crown and sewed with twine. Meat is trimmed from the ends of the ribs. Meaty eye of the rib exposed at base. Rib ends may be decorated the same as in French roast.
Roast.

HOLLYWOOD FILET

Formed by combining Saratoga roll and boneless rib section in a skewered roll and slicing approximately one and one-half inches thick.
Broil, grill.

LOIN ROAST

Contains the backbone and muscles, including the loin, tenderloin, and flank. Tenderloin is separated from loin by the finger bones. Kidney fat covers top of tenderloin and fat covers surface of roast.
Roast.

LOIN ROAST (BONELESS)

Full loin with the backbone removed, fashioned into a roll and tied with twine. Muscles include the loin, tenderloin, and flank. Fat interspersed in roast and covers outer surface.
Roast.

ENGLISH CHOPS
Loin section may be kept whole and
sliced across entire loin section to form a
double loin or English chop.
Broil, pan-broil, pan-fry.

LOIN CHOPS
The loin section may be split down
backbone of animal and sliced for single
loin chops or kept whole and sliced across
entire loin section to form a double loin
or English chop.
Broil, pan-broil, pan-fry.

SIRLOIN ROAST
Tender section cut from upper portion
of lamb leg. Contains backbone
and part of hip bone.
Roast.

SIRLOIN STEAKS
Cut from the sirloin section of the lamb
leg. Contains backbone and part of hip
bone which varies in shape with each
chop. Muscles include the top sirloin,
tenderloin and flank. Fat on outside, fell
removed.
Broil, pan-broil, pan-fry.

FRENCH LEG
Contains tailbone, part of hip bone, leg and shank bones. Muscles include outside and inside knuckle, sirloin and heel. Small amount of meat trimmed from above break joint.
Roast.

SHANK HALF LEG
Lower half of leg contains same muscle and bones as French leg except that the shank bone has not been Frenched.
Roast.

SIRLOIN HALF LEG
Includes sirloin section and upper half of a full leg. Carving is simplified by loosening aitch bone (hip bone).
Roast.

2-IN-1 LEG COMBINATION
Full leg with the sirloin section cut into chops or steaks for one meal. Three-quarter leg may be roasted for a second meal.
Chops: broil, pan-broil, pan-fry.
Roast larger portion.

BONELESS LEG
Full leg with bones removed. Meat rolled
and tied securely for roasting in
oven or rotisserie.
Oven-roast, spit-roast.

ROUND (LEG) STEAK
Lean meaty slices usually cut from
center of leg. Contains round bone.
Braise.

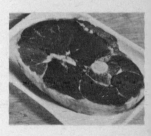

Carving Instructions

ROAST LEG OF LAMB

1. To simplify the carving of the sirloin portion of the leg, have your butcher loosen the aitch bone (hip) cutting through the ball-socket joint.

2. Place leg of lamb before carver so thick meaty section is on foreside of platter. (Right leg is shown in illustration. A left leg would be placed with leg bone to left.) Insert fork firmly in large end of leg and cut two or three lengthwise slices from side nearest carver.

3. Turn leg so it rests firmly on cut surface. Hold roast firmly with inserted fork, and beginning at shank end, make slices down to leg bone. Continue to make parallel slices until aitch bone at large end is reached.

4. With fork still in place, the knife is run parallel to the leg bone to free the slices.

RACK OF LAMB ROAST
The carver inserts a fork into the left end
of the rack. With a sharp knife held in
the right hand he cuts down between
the ribs with clean strokes, serving either
one or two chop portions per person. If
left-handed, insert fork in right end, carve
with left. If rack is from a small animal
it will be easier to carve if placed flat on
the platter, fat-side up, as the small racks
may not stand on end well.

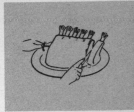

CROWN ROAST OF LAMB
The carver will need a silver serving spoon
for the dressing if the crown is stuffed,
as well as the usual carving knife and fork.
Insert fork into left side of crown at an
angle to steady it. A sharp knife will glide
down between the rib bones easily and
cleanly. Cut one or two rib portions per
person, placing a serving of meat and a
spoonful of dressing on each plate.

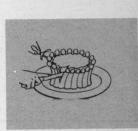

PRECARVED LAMB SHOULDER ROAST
All carving is already done for you. Just
cut the tie-strings and serve. When you
shop, select a precarved lamb shoulder
roast or ask your meat man to prepare it
for you. So easy—so good!

ROAST SQUARE SHOULDER
Because of flat bones, carve in chunks
instead of slicing.

Timetable
for Cooking Lamb

❧❧❧❧❧❧❧❧ ❧❧❧❧❧❧❧ ❧❧❧❧❧❧

*Lamb is very easy to cook and may be prepared by any of the
basic cookery methods used in preparing other red meats. As a
guide and for handy general reference, however, the following
table will be useful.*

*When cooking lamb from the frozen state, allow from one
third to one half more cooking time. For a special taste treat try
lamb cooked less well done than below. See internal temperature
recommendations on page nine.*

Oven-roasted at 325° F. to an internal temperature of 175° to 180° F.		Broiled*	Braised	Simmered
Cut	Minutes per Pound	Total Time in Minutes	Total Time	Total Time
Leg (bone-in)	30–35			
Boneless, rolled or netted	35–40			
Shoulder (bone-in)	30–35			
Boneless, rolled or netted	40–45			
Cushion	30–35			

* Pan-broiling and/or griddle-broiling require approximately one-half as
much time as broiling.

Breast (stuffed)	30–35		1½–2 hrs.
Rolled			1½–2 hrs.
Riblets			1½–2 hrs.
Lamb Loaf	30–35		
Shoulder Chops (1 inch)		12	¾–1 hr.
(1½ inch)		18	1–1¼ hrs.
(2 inch)		22	1–1½ hrs.
Rib Chops (1 inch)		12	
(1½ inch)		18	
(2 inch)		22	
Loin Chops (1 inch)		12	
(1½ inch)		18	
(2 inch)		22	
Lamb Patties (1"x3")		18	
Neck Slices (¾")			1 hr.
Shanks			1½–2 hrs.
Cubes (1–1½")			1½–2 hrs. 1½–2 hrs.
Crown Roast	30–35		
Rack	30–35		

Hors d'Oeuvres and Canapés

❧❧❧❧❧❧❧ ❧❧❧❧❧❧❧ ❧❧❧❧

Tasty hot and cold appetizers provide a festive note which sets the tone for special predinner cocktail hours. They provide an excellent way to use ground leftover roast lamb and prove how versatile this fine meat can be. Riblets in barbecue sauce are also excellent.

Lamb Roll-Ups

Makes 8 roll-ups

1 cup chopped cooked lamb	1 teaspoon garlic salt
¼ cup mayonnaise	Dash cayenne
1 tablespoon prepared horseradish	8 slices bread
	2 tablespoons melted butter

Combine lamb, mayonnaise, horseradish, garlic salt, and cayenne. Mix well. Trim crusts from bread. Spread with lamb mixture; roll up. Brush with butter. Place seamside down on baking sheet. Bake in oven at 400° for 10 to 12 minutes, or until lightly browned.

✿

Lamb-and-Cheese Pinwheels

Makes 36 hors d'oeuvres

2 cups sifted all-purpose flour
1 teaspoon salt
½ cup grated Cheddar cheese
⅔ cup shortening
⅓ cup cold water
¼ cup mayonnaise
1 pound ground lamb
½ teaspoon rosemary
½ teaspoon salt
⅛ teaspoon pepper

Combine flour and salt; add cheese and mix lightly. Cut in shortening. Add water and mix lightly. Press into ball. Roll out on lightly floured surface into 12 x 18-inch rectangle. Spread with mayonnaise. Combine remaining ingredients; mix well. Spread lamb mixture over mayonnaise. Roll up jelly-roll fashion. Cut into ½-inch slices. Place on ungreased baking sheets. Bake in oven at 425° about 15 minutes, or until pastry is lightly browned.

❖

Lamb-Stuffed Mushrooms

Makes 3 dozen

2 cups ground cooked lamb
1 tablespoon finely chopped chives
1 tablespoon prepared horseradish
⅓ cup mayonnaise
Salt and pepper to taste
3 dozen medium-sized mushroom caps (about 1½ pounds)

Combine lamb, chives, horseradish, mayonnaise, and salt and pepper; mix well. Fill mushroom caps with lamb mixture. Arrange in buttered shallow baking dish. Bake in oven at 350° for 20 minutes.

❖

Tiny Lamb Appetizers in Wine Cream Sauce

Makes 6 to 8 servings

1 pound ground lamb
1 cup grated apple
1/4 cup finely chopped onion
1 teaspoon salt
1/8 teaspoon pepper

1 cup commercial sour cream
1/2 cup rosé
1/3 cup chopped pimiento-stuffed green olives

Combine lamb, apple, onion, salt, and pepper; mix well. Shape into 3/4-inch balls. Cook over low heat 30 minutes, or until browned on all sides. Drain off drippings. Combine remaining ingredients; mix well. Pour over lamb balls. Heat to serving temperature over low heat.

❁

Lamb-and-Cheese Canapé Spread

Makes about 2 cups

1 pound ground lamb
1 clove garlic, crushed
1 package (3 ounces) cream cheese, softened
2 tablespoons chili sauce

1 tablespoon prepared horseradish
1 teaspoon salt
1/8 teaspoon pepper

Combine lamb and garlic. Cook over low heat until browned, stirring occasionally. Drain off drippings. Combine lamb and remaining ingredients; mix well. Chill. Serve as a spread for bread or crackers, as desired.

❁

Lamb-Olive Appetizers

Makes 16 appetizers

1 pound ground lamb
¾ cup chopped onion
1 small clove garlic,
crushed
⅓ cup chopped pimiento-
stuffed green olives

1 cup heavy cream
2 cups biscuit mix
⅓ cup grated Parmesan
cheese

Cook lamb, onion, and garlic over medium heat until lamb
is browned, stirring occasionally. Drain off drippings. Add
olives to lamb mixture and mix well. Reserve 2 tablespoons
cream. Combine remaining cream, biscuit mix, and
Parmesan cheese; mix well. Press into a ball and roll out
on lightly floured surface to 16-inch square. Cut into sixteen
4-inch squares. Place lamb mixture in center of pastry.
Fold in corners and seal edges. Shape into 2½-inch balls;
flatten slightly. Place, seamside down, on baking sheets.
Brush with remaining cream. Bake in oven at 400° for
20 minutes.

❁

Grecian Pinwheel Appetizers

Makes 3 dozen appetizers

1 tablespoon crushed
mint leaves
1 package (10 ounces)
piecrust mix
1 pound ground lamb

1 can (3 ounces) chopped
mushrooms, drained
and finely chopped
¼ cup chopped parsley
½ teaspoon salt
⅛ teaspoon pepper

Add mint leaves to piecrust mix and prepare crust, following package directions. Roll out to 12 x 18-inch rectangle. Combine lamb, mushrooms, parsley, salt, and pepper; mix lightly. Spread lamb mixture evenly over top of dough; roll up jelly-roll fashion, starting at longest side. Cut into ½-inch slices. Bake on ungreased baking sheet in hot 425° oven 15 minutes or until lightly browned. Serve immediately.

❁

Lamb Meat Balls with Madeira Sauce

Makes 4 to 6 servings

1 pound ground lamb	2 tablespoons chopped chives
1 egg, beaten	
⅓ cup fine dry bread crumbs	2 tablespoons butter or margarine
¼ cup chopped parsley	½ cup Madeira
1 teaspoon salt	1 chicken-bouillon cube
¼ teaspoon pepper	1 teaspoon paprika
½ teaspoon rosemary	Lemon slices

Combine lamb, egg, crumbs, parsley, salt, pepper, rosemary, and chives; mix well. Shape into 1-inch balls. Melt butter in skillet. Add lamb balls and cook over low heat until browned on all sides. Drain off fat. Add Madeira, bouillon cube, and paprika; mix well. Cover and cook 20 minutes, stirring frequently. Serve lamb balls in Madeira sauce from chafing dish, as desired. Garnish with lemon-slice twists.

❁

Dolmas (Stuffed Grape Leaves)

Makes 50 servings

1 pound ground lamb
1 large onion, finely
chopped
½ cup uncooked rice
½ cup parsley and mint,
finely chopped
2 teaspoons salt

Pepper to taste
3 tablespoons butter
50 grape leaves (fresh or
canned)
Avgolemono Sauce II (see
below)

Mix all ingredients except butter and grape leaves. If meat
is too sticky to form ball easily, add a little water and
mix well.

Drain the grape leaves and rinse with water. Measure
about a teaspoonful of meat mixture to form a ball. Place in
corner of grape leaf and wrap leaf around ball so that
no meat is exposed.

Place these in a pan with enough water to cover bottom
of pan. Top with butter and boil 20 to 25 minutes until
rice is cooked. These may be served with Avgolemono
Sauce II. (Avgolemono Sauce I, p. 89, is slightly
different and not appropriate here.)

Avgolemono Sauce II

3 eggs
Juice of 1 lemon

½ cup liquid from cooked
grape leaves

Beat eggs until frothy; add the juice of lemon slowly,
stirring constantly. Then add liquid from grape leaves
a little at a time, stirring constantly so that egg won't
curdle. If sauce seems watery, place in saucepan over
very low flame and simmer, stirring constantly, until
desired consistency is reached.

Lamb Luncheon Platter

Makes 4 servings

1 tablespoon mayonnaise
3 tablespoons vinegar
2 tablespoons catsup
½ teaspoon salt
¼ teaspoon marjoram
½ pound cooked sliced
lamb

8 ounces sliced Muenster
cheese
4 deviled eggs
Radish roses
Ripe olives
Tomato slices

Mix together mayonnaise, vinegar, catsup, salt, and
marjoram. Arrange remaining ingredients on platter;
serve with the herb dressing.

❃

Miniature Barquettes of Spiced Lamb

Makes about 12 servings

3 onions, finely chopped
½ cup butter
1 pound cooked lamb,
finely chopped
½ cup golden seedless
raisins
½ cup pine nuts
¼ cup dried currants

2 tablespoons tomato
paste
2 cloves garlic, finely
chopped
½ cup chopped parsley
Barquettes (small oval tart
shells)°
Crisp fried chopped onions

Sauté finely chopped onions in butter until brown. Add
lamb, raisins, pine nuts, currants, tomato paste, and garlic;
mix well. Add parsley. Spoon into barquettes. Sprinkle
tops with fried onions.

° Recipe is sufficient for 12 or more barquettes depending upon size of
barquettes used.

❃

Lamb Three-Cornered Hats

Makes 16 hors d'oeuvres

1 cup sifted all-purpose flour
Dash salt
⅓ cup shortening
½ cup grated Cheddar cheese
¼ cup water
1 can (3 ounces) sliced mushrooms
¼ cup stock or bouillon

2 tablespoons butter
2 tablespoons flour
1 cup finely chopped cooked lamb
¼ cup finely chopped onion
¼ teaspoon Worcestershire sauce
¾ teaspoon salt
¼ teaspoon pepper

Sift together 1 cup flour and dash salt. Cut in shortening. Add cheese and water; mix lightly. Press into ball. Roll out on lightly floured surface to ⅛-inch thickness. Cut with floured 3-inch cutter into 16 circles. Chill.

Meanwhile, drain mushrooms; reserve liquid. Combine mushroom liquid and stock. Melt butter and add 2 tablespoons flour; blend. Gradually add stock mixture. Cook and stir over medium heat until thickened. Add mushrooms, lamb, onion, Worcestershire, ¾ teaspoon salt, and pepper. Mix well. Cool.

Place lamb mixture in centers of pastry circles. Pinch edges to form three corners. Place on baking sheet. Bake in oven at 375° for 25 to 30 minutes.

❖

Lamb Hors d'Oeuvre Meat Balls

Makes 8 servings

- **2 pounds ground lamb**
- **2 teaspoons salt**
- **½ teaspoon pepper**
- **2 tablespoons chopped parsley**
- **¼ cup salad oil**
- **2 cloves garlic, crushed**
- **2 cans (8 ounces each) tomato sauce**
- **2 cans (6 ounces each) tomato paste**
- **1 cup water**
- **1 teaspoon grated Parmesan cheese**
- **½ teaspoon onion salt**
- **¾ teaspoon basil**
- **½ teaspoon oregano**
- **⅛ teaspoon crushed red pepper**
- **Parsley**

Combine lamb, 1 teaspoon salt, ¼ teaspoon pepper, and 2 tablespoons chopped parsley; mix well. Shape lamb mixture into 1-inch balls. Heat oil. Add lamb meat balls and cook until browned on all sides. Remove lamb meat balls; reserve ¼ cup drippings. Add garlic and lamb meat balls to lamb drippings and cook over low heat 5 minutes, stirring occasionally. Combine tomato sauce, tomato paste, water, remaining salt and pepper, cheese, onion salt, basil, oregano, and red pepper; mix well. Add tomato sauce mixture to lamb and cook 30 minutes, stirring occasionally. Garnish with parsley. Serve with picks.

Appetizer Lamb Meat Balls

Makes about 36 meat balls

3 tablespoons salad oil
1½ cups chopped onion
3 pounds ground lamb
3 eggs, beaten
3 cups fine soft bread
crumbs
3 tablespoons chopped
parsley

1 tablespoon chopped
mint or dehydrated
mint leaves
1 tablespoon salt
¾ teaspoon pepper
1½ cups unbleached flour
1 cup salad oil

Heat 3 tablespoons oil. Add onion and cook slowly until tender. Remove from heat. Add lamb, eggs, crumbs, parsley, mint, salt, and pepper; mix well. Shape into small balls. Coat with flour. Heat 1 cup oil. Add lamb balls and cook until browned on all sides. Cover and cook 30 minutes over low heat.

❄

Sherried Lamb in Patty Shells

Makes 6 servings

¼ cup sliced scallions
¼ pound mushrooms,
sliced
¼ cup butter or
margarine
¼ cup flour
1½ teaspoons salt
¼ teaspoon rosemary
⅛ teaspoon pepper
¾ cup milk

1 cup light cream
2 cups diced cooked
lamb
2 tablespoons diced
canned pimiento
2 tablespoons dry sherry
1 package (10 ounces)
frozen patty shells,
prepared according to
package directions

Sauté scallions and mushrooms in butter until tender. Stir in flour and seasonings. Gradually add milk and cream; cook, stirring constantly, until sauce thickens and boils. Add lamb, pimiento and sherry; mix and heat thoroughly. Spoon into hot patty shells on serving plate. Garnish as desired.

❄

Pâté of Lamb

Makes about 12 servings

2 pounds finely ground lamb
2½ teaspoons salt
1 teaspoon pepper
1 large onion, grated
¾ pound cracked wheat
3 cups cold water
1½ cups diced cooked lamb

¾ cup chopped onion
2 cloves garlic
½ teaspoon thyme
¾ cup pine nuts
2 tablespoons butter
Melted butter

Combine ground lamb with salt, pepper, and grated onion; blend well. Soften cracked wheat in water; rinse and drain well. Mix with ground lamb. Put mixture through food grinder. Take one-half of mixture and spread in well-buttered shallow baking pan. Brown diced lamb, chopped onion, garlic, thyme, and pine nuts in 2 tablespoons butter. Spread this mixture over lamb-and-wheat paste. Cover with remaining lamb-and-wheat paste. Pour melted butter over top and bake in slow (325°) oven for 30 minutes. Cut into small squares and serve very hot.

❄

Western Lamb Riblets

Makes 12 servings

3 pounds lamb riblets
1 can (6 ounces) tomato
   paste
½ cup catsup
¼ cup vinegar
¼ cup molasses

1 medium-sized onion,
   sliced
1 teaspoon salt
¼ teaspoon pepper
⅛ teaspoon Tabasco

Place lamb riblets on rack in shallow roasting pan. Bake in 325° oven for about 1½ hours. Drain off drippings. Combine remaining ingredients; mix well. Pour and brush some of sauce over riblets. Continue baking for 1½ hours more, basting occasionally with sauce. Turn riblets twice, if desired, to coat underside.

NOTE: This recipe may be used as a main dish as well as an appetizer.

✱

Soups

SOUP STOCK

Stock for soup can be made from several parts of the lamb, but neck slices are recommended particularly, since they are meaty enough to provide good flavor, and are easy to use and inexpensive. The following recipe may be considered fairly basic when making lamb stock for Scotch broth or other soups.

Lamb Lentil Soup

Makes 6 to 8 servings

- 1 cup dried lentils
- 1 pound shoulder of lamb, diced
- 4 slices bacon, chopped
- 2 medium-sized onions, sliced
- 1½ cups diced carrots
- 2 teaspoons salt
- ¼ teaspoon pepper
- 1½ quarts stock or bouillon

Cover lentils with cold water and let stand 2 hours; drain. Cook lamb, bacon, and onions over medium heat until lamb is browned, stirring occasionally. Add lentils and remaining ingredients. Cover and cook 3 hours over low heat, stirring occasionally.

Stock for Lamb Soup

Makes 3 quarts

3 whole lamb necks,
trimmed of excess fat,
and cut in pieces (do
not discard bones)

3½ quarts water (to cover)
1½ teaspoons salt
½ teaspoon pepper
2 onions, sliced

Place lamb necks in deep kettle, cover with water, add salt, pepper, and onions, and allow to simmer three to four hours. Strain, cool, and chill stock.

If you wish, the cooked meat can be trimmed from the neck bones and added to the stock for use in certain recipes.

If you prefer a completely fat-free stock, refrigerate the liquid long enough for fat to rise to the top and congeal so that it can be lifted off and disposed of.

Use for any recipe requiring stock.

❊

Lamb Onion Soup

Makes about 2½ quarts

¼ cup butter
1 pound diced shoulder
of lamb
1 quart sliced onion
2 quarts stock or bouillon

2 teaspoons salt
¼ teaspoon pepper
1 teaspoon rosemary
2 tablespoons cornstarch
¼ cup water

Melt butter; add lamb and onion and cook over medium heat 10 minutes, stirring occasionally. Add stock or bouillon, salt, pepper, and rosemary; mix well. Cover and cook over medium heat 1 hour, stirring occasionally. Blend cornstarch with water. Add to onion mixture and cook 10 minutes, stirring frequently.

❊

Lamb-and-Vegetable Soup

Makes 4 servings

- 1 pound shoulder of lamb, cut into 1½-inch cubes
- 1 quart water
- 1 package (2½ ounces) dehydrated tomato-vegetable soup mix
- ½ cup commercial sour cream
- 2 tablespoons chopped chives

Cook lamb over low heat until browned on all sides. Add water; heat to boiling point. Add soup mix. Cover and cook 30 minutes over low heat, stirring occasionally. Serve topped with sour cream and chives.

❁

Lamb-and-Barley Tomato Soup

Makes 6 servings

- 1 pound lamb shoulder, cubed
- ½ cup chopped onion
- 2 cups stock or bouillon
- 1 can (1 pound, 13 ounces) tomatoes
- 1 can (8 ounces) tomato sauce
- ¼ cup firmly packed brown sugar
- ½ cup barley
- ¼ teaspoon rosemary
- Salt and pepper to taste
- ¼ cup chopped parsley

Cook lamb cubes and chopped onion until lamb is browned well. Add stock or bouillon, the tomatoes, tomato sauce, brown sugar, barley, rosemary, and salt and pepper. Cover and cook 45 minutes over low heat, stirring occasionally. Add chopped parsley.

❁

Lamb-and-Rice Soup

Makes 6 servings

2 tablespoons butter
1 pound shoulder of lamb, diced
2 medium-sized onions, sliced
1 medium-sized green pepper, cut in strips
1 cup chopped celery

1½ quarts stock or bouillon
2 teaspoons curry powder
½ teaspoon basil
2 teaspoons salt
¼ teaspoon pepper
⅓ cup rice

Melt butter; add lamb, onions, green pepper, and celery, and cook over low heat until lamb is browned on all sides. Add stock or bouillon, curry powder, basil, salt, and pepper; mix well. Cover and cook 30 minutes over low heat, stirring occasionally. Add rice and cover, and cook 20 minutes.

❖

Lamb & Corn Chowder

Makes 8 servings

¼ cup butter
2 pounds lamb shoulder, cut into ¾-inch cubes
2 cups chopped onion
1 large clove garlic, crushed
Salt and pepper to taste
1 teaspoon dry mustard

⅛ teaspoon cayenne
2 cans (1 pound) whole-kernel corn
3⅓ cups (2 large cans) undiluted evaporated milk
2 teaspoons paprika

Melt butter; add lamb and cook over low heat until browned, stirring occasionally. Add onion, garlic, salt and pepper, mustard and cayenne, and cook 5 minutes. Add undrained corn and cook, covered, 20 minutes over low heat. Add evaporated milk and cook 10 minutes, stirring occasionally. Sprinkle with paprika before serving.

❄

Pigeon Pea Soup

Makes 6 servings

2 tablespoons salad oil
1½ pounds diced lamb
    shoulder
6 cups hot water
1 can (8 ounces) tomato
    sauce
1 medium-sized onion,
    chopped
2 green peppers,
    chopped

1 medium-sized tomato,
    chopped
1 large clove garlic,
    crushed
⅛ teaspoon whole
    coriander seed
1 cup uncooked rice
2 teaspoons salt
⅛ teaspoon pepper
1 can (1 pound) pigeon
    peas

Heat oil; add lamb and cook over low heat until browned on all sides. Drain off drippings, if necessary. Add water, tomato sauce, onion, green peppers, tomato, garlic, and coriander seed. Cover and cook over low heat 30 minutes. Add rice, salt, pepper, and undrained peas. Stir well. Cover and cook 12 minutes over low heat, or until rice and lamb are tender.

❄

Favorite Lamb-and-Barley Soup

Makes 6 to 8 servings

1 tablespoon shortening
1½ pounds lamb shoulder, cubed
1 cup sliced onions
1 cup sliced celery
1 medium-sized green pepper, diced
2 quarts stock or bouillon
1½ cups diced potatoes
1½ cups cut whole-kernel corn
1 teaspoon salt
⅛ teaspoon pepper
¼ teaspoon thyme
½ cup barley

Melt shortening in kettle. Add lamb, onions, celery, and green pepper. Cook over low heat until lamb is browned on all sides, stirring occasionally. Add stock or bouillon. Heat to boiling point. Add remaining ingredients. Cover and cook over low heat, stirring occasionally, for 45 minutes or until vegetables are tender.

❁

Lamb-Vegetable Soup

Makes 4 servings

2 tablespoons butter
1 pound lamb shoulder, diced
1 medium-sized onion, sliced
1 medium-sized green pepper, chopped
3 cups stock or bouillon
1 package (10 ounces) frozen mixed vegetables
1 canned pimiento, diced
1 can (8 ounces) tomato sauce
1 teaspoon salt
¼ teaspoon pepper

Melt butter; add lamb and cook until browned on all sides. Add onion and green pepper and cook 5 minutes. Add stock or bouillon, cover and cook 25 minutes. Add remaining ingredients; mix well. Cover and cook 10 minutes, or until vegetables are tender.

❋

Quick Lamb Soup

Makes 4 servings

1 tablespoon shortening	1 bunch carrots, pared and cut into 2-inch pieces
¾ pound lamb shoulder, diced	
4½ cups water	1 can (1 pound) white onions
3 chicken-bouillon cubes	
1½ teaspoons salt	1 package (10 ounces) frozen green beans
Pepper to taste	
½ teaspoon rosemary	½ cup packaged precooked rice

Melt shortening in kettle. Cook lamb until browned; drain off drippings. Add water, bouillon cubes, salt, pepper, rosemary, and carrots. Cover and cook 40 minutes over low heat. Add undrained onions and green beans and cook 5 minutes, or until beans are tender. Add rice; mix well to moisten. Remove from heat and cover. Let stand 15 minutes.

❋

Lamb-Mushroom Soup

Makes 4 servings

½ pound ground lamb
¼ cup fine dry bread crumbs
⅛ teaspoon allspice
¼ teaspoon cinnamon
½ teaspoon salt
⅛ teaspoon pepper

2 tablespoons butter
2 cans (10½ ounces) condensed cream of mushroom soup
2 cups milk
Lemon rind

Combine lamb, bread crumbs, allspice, cinnamon, salt, and pepper; mix well. Shape into ¾-inch balls. Melt butter; add lamb meat balls, and cook over low heat until browned on all sides. Add mushroom soup and milk; mix well. Cover and cook 20 minutes over low heat. Garnish with lemon rind before serving.

❉

Lamb Salads and Cold Platters

Hearty luncheon salads are popular summer and winter. While most people are accustomed to fish, seafood, and chicken salads for lunch, not everyone thinks about using lamb in salads.

Here are some delicious treats you're sure to like. They provide just one more way to use leftover roast lamb.

Lamb Salad Supreme

Makes 4 servings

- **2 cups diced cooked lamb**
- **1 cucumber, sliced**
- **2 tomatoes, sliced**
- **4 cups torn lettuce**
- **1/2 cup commercial sour cream**

Combine above ingredients except sour cream. Chill until ready to serve. Add the sour cream and toss lightly.

Lamb & Rice Salad

Makes 6 servings

3 cups cold cooked rice
2 cups cubed cooked lamb
½ cup chopped red onion
¼ cup chopped parsley
1 medium-sized tomato, diced
½ cup bottled Italian salad dressing
3 tablespoons lemon juice
Salt and pepper
Salad greens

Combine all ingredients except salad greens in bowl. Mix well and chill. Serve on salad greens, if desired.

❁

Almond Lamb Salad

Makes 4 to 5 servings

2 cups cooked diced lamb
½ cup slivered almonds, toasted
1½ cups diced celery
1 cup salad dressing or mayonnaise
2 tablespoons lemon juice
1 teaspoon salt

Combine lamb, almonds and celery. Mix together remaining ingredients. Add dressing to lamb and mix well. Serve chilled.

NOTE: If desired, serve warm. Grate cheese over the top. Crumble potato chips and sprinkle over all. Place in 350° oven until heated through (about 20 minutes).

❁

Indian Lamb Salad

Makes 4 to 5 servings

2 cups cooked diced
lamb
⅓ cup shredded coconut
1¼ cups thinly sliced
celery

2 medium-sized oranges,
sectioned
Curry dressing or Tropical
dressing (see below)

Combine lamb, coconut, celery, and oranges. Add dressing
to lamb and toss well.

❁

Curry Dressing

¾ cup mayonnaise or
salad dressing
1½ tablespoons wine
vinegar

1 teaspoon salt
1¾ teaspoons curry
powder
¼ teaspoon pepper

Combine ingredients and mix well.

Tropical Dressing

½ cup mayonnaise or
salad dressing
½ cup commercial sour
cream

2 tablespoons lemon juice
1 teaspoon salt
¼ teaspoon nutmeg
¼ teaspoon allspice

Combine ingredients and mix well.

❁

Lamb Macaroni Salad

Makes 6 servings

2 cups cooked diced lamb
3 cups cooked shell
 macaroni
½ cup chopped sweet
 pickle
1 cup diced celery
⅓ cup chopped onion
1 cup grated Cheddar
 cheese

1 cup salad dressing or
 mayonnaise
1 tablespoon red wine
 vinegar
1 teaspoon prepared
 mustard
1 teaspoon salt
¼ teaspoon pepper
Dash cayenne

Combine lamb, macaroni, pickle, celery, onion, and cheese.
Combine salad dressing, vinegar, and seasonings. Add to
lamb-macaroni mixture and toss well.

❊

Lamb Waldorf Salad

Makes 5 servings

2 cups cooked diced
 lamb
1½ cups grape halves
1½ cups diced apple
1 cup chopped walnuts
½ cup commercial sour
 cream

½ cup mayonnaise or
 salad dressing
2 tablespoons wine
 vinegar
1 teaspoon salt
¼ teaspoon pepper
¼ teaspoon paprika
⅛ teaspoon cayenne

Combine lamb, grapes, apple, and walnuts. Mix together
remaining ingredients for salad dressing. Add dressing
to lamb mixture and toss well.

❊

Lamb Salad, Eastern Style

Makes 6 servings

2 cups ground cooked
lamb
1 cup cooked rice
⅓ cup chopped chutney
½ teaspoon curry powder

1½ cups chopped celery
Dash salt
½ cup mayonnaise
Crisp salad greens

Combine lamb, rice, chutney, curry powder, celery, and salt. Add mayonnaise; toss lightly. Serve on salad greens.

✦

Lamb Vegetable Salad

Makes 6 servings

2 cups cooked lamb, cut
into ½-inch cubes
2 cups diced cooked
potatoes
1 cup grated carrots
½ cup sliced scallions
¾ cup diced green pepper
½ cup sliced radishes

1 medium-sized
cucumber, halved
lengthwise and sliced
1 clove garlic, crushed
1 cup commercial sour
cream
½ cup French dressing
1 teaspoon seasoned salt
¼ teaspoon pepper
Chicory or lettuce

Combine lamb, potatoes, carrots, scallions, green pepper, radishes, and cucumber. Toss lightly but thoroughly. Combine garlic, sour cream, French dressing, seasoned salt, and pepper; mix well. Pour over lamb mixture. Toss lightly but thoroughly. Arrange lamb mixture on bed of chicory or lettuce.

✦

Slimmer's Salad

Makes 4 to 6 servings

1 tablespoon instant minced onion

2 tablespoons chopped parsley

1½ teaspoons salt

¼ teaspoon pepper

3 tablespoons salad or olive oil

⅓ cup vinegar

½ teaspoon crushed oregano

1 pound cooked lamb shoulder, diced

3 cups torn chicory or Western iceberg lettuce

2 medium-sized tomatoes, diced

1 cup chopped celery

1 cup sliced cooked potatoes

Combine onion, parsley, salt, pepper, oil, vinegar, and oregano; mix well. Add lamb and mix well. Chill 1 hour, turning lamb occasionally. Meanwhile, combine remaining ingredients; toss lightly. Chill. Add lamb mixture to salad-greens mixture and toss lightly but thoroughly.

❁

Lamb Salad Plate

Makes 6 servings

½ cup French dressing

¼ cup lemon juice

¼ cup finely chopped onion

1 teaspoon paprika

6 slices cooked lamb shoulder

Combine French dressing, lemon juice, onion, and paprika; mix well. Add lamb. Chill 2 hours; turn lamb occasionally during chilling period. Serve lamb with cole slaw, tomato wedges, and gelatin salads, as desired.

❁

Lamb Salad Continental

Makes 4 servings

½ cup commercial sour
   cream
¼ cup mayonnaise
½ teaspoon salt
⅛ teaspoon pepper
¼ teaspoon dill seed
1 tablespoon vinegar

2 cups (about ½ pound)
   diced cooked lamb
½ cup chopped celery
1 canned pimiento,
   chopped
Lettuce

Mix sour cream, mayonnaise, salt, pepper, dill seed, and
vinegar in bowl. Add lamb, celery, and pimiento; toss and
mix thoroughly. Serve lamb salad on lettuce.

❂

Cold Lamb & Vegetable Platter

Makes 4 servings

⅔ cup vinegar
⅓ cup salad oil
1 tablespoon sugar
1 teaspoon salt
¼ teaspoon pepper
⅓ cup chopped parsley
½ teaspoon basil
⅛ teaspoon celery seed

1 can (1 pound) potatoes,
   drained
1 large onion, sliced
1 medium-sized
   cucumber, sliced
4 large slices cooked lamb
   shoulder or leg

Combine vinegar, oil, sugar, salt, pepper, parsley, basil,
and celery seed; blend or shake well. Add remaining
ingredients. Chill 2 to 3 hours, turning vegetables and
lamb occasionally. Remove potatoes, onion, cucumber,
and lamb from vinegar mixture. Arrange on platter.

❂

Lamb Salad

Makes 4 servings

1 tablespoon dehydrated minced onion
2 tablespoons chopped parsley
1½ teaspoons salt
¼ teaspoon pepper
3 tablespoons salad or olive oil
⅓ cup vinegar
½ teaspoon oregano

1 pound cooked lamb shoulder, diced
3 cups torn chicory or lettuce
2 medium-sized tomatoes, diced
1 cup chopped celery
1 can (8 ounces) potatoes, drained and sliced

Combine onion, parsley, salt, pepper, oil, vinegar, and oregano; mix well. Add lamb and mix well. Chill 1 hour, turning lamb occasionally. Meanwhile, combine remaining ingredients; toss lightly. Chill. Add lamb mixture to chicory or lettuce mixture and toss lightly but thoroughly.

❄

Spanish Lamb Salad

Makes 6 servings

⅓ cup olive oil
¼ cup lemon juice
2 tablespoons vinegar
1 tablespoon fresh chopped chives
½ teaspoon salt
½ teaspoon basil
⅛ teaspoon pepper

3 cups slivered cooked lamb
½ cup sliced pimiento-stuffed olives
1 small green pepper
2 medium-sized tomatoes, diced
2 hard-cooked eggs, sliced
Lettuce

Blend oil, lemon juice, vinegar, chives, and seasonings. Chill. Arrange lamb, olives, green pepper, tomatoes and eggs in lettuce-lined bowl. Pour dressing on top and toss.

❁

Lamb Luncheon Salad

Makes 4 servings

1 package (10 ounces) frozen Brussels sprouts
1 cup salad oil
1/2 cup lemon juice
1 teaspoon basil
1/4 teaspoon rosemary
1 teaspoon seasoned salt
1 teaspoon dehydrated minced onion

2 cups (about 1/2 pound) sliced mushrooms
1 pound cooked lamb shoulder, diced
1 large tomato, cut into wedges
1 cup diced Swiss cheese (1-inch cubes)
1/2 cup thin carrot strips
Crisp lettuce

Cook Brussels sprouts according to package directions; drain if necessary. Combine oil, lemon juice, basil, rosemary, seasoned salt, and onion; shake or blend well. Heat oil mixture. Pour oil mixture over mushrooms. Add Brussels sprouts and remaining ingredients; mix well. Chill 2 hours, stirring occasionally. Drain lamb, cheese, and vegetables; reserve oil mixture. Arrange lamb, cheese, and vegetables on lettuce. Serve with oil mixture.

❁

Tossed Lamb Salad

Makes 4 to 6 servings

3 cups diced cooked lamb
¼ cup clear French dressing
4 teaspoons lemon juice
1 cup diced celery
⅓ cup diced green pepper
2 tablespoons chopped onion

2 tablespoons chopped pimiento
1 tablespoon capers
¼ teaspoon garlic salt
¼ teaspoon curry powder
¼ cup mayonnaise
2 ounces (about ¼ cup) Blue cheese, crumbled
Torn salad greens

Mix lamb with French dressing and lemon juice; chill.
Combine remaining ingredients; toss together. Chill.
Serve with additional dressing, if desired.

❋

Greek Lamb-and-Olive Salad

Makes 4 servings

½ cup olive oil
½ cup wine vinegar
2 tablespoons commercial mixed salad herbs
1 teaspoon crushed mint leaves
2 cups cooked slivered lamb

2 medium-sized cucumbers, peeled and sliced
2 medium-sized tomatoes, diced
½ cup black olives

Combine oil, vinegar, salad seasoning, and mint. Pour
over lamb and marinate several hours. Combine with
remaining ingredients; toss well or arrange on chicory,
if desired.

❋

Lamb Salad Julienne

Makes 4 servings

½ cup commercial sour
cream
¼ cup mayonnaise
½ teaspoon salt
⅛ teaspoon pepper
¼ teaspoon dill seed
1 tablespoon vinegar

2 cups (about ½ pound)
diced cooked lamb
½ cup chopped celery
1 canned pimiento,
chopped
Lettuce

Mix sour cream, mayonnaise, salt, pepper, dill seed, and
vinegar in bowl. Add lamb, celery and pimiento; toss
and mix thoroughly. Serve lamb salad on lettuce.

❂

Spring Lamb Salad

Makes 6 servings

1 package (10 ounces)
frozen black-eyed peas
2 strips bacon, cooked
until crisp, and
crumbled
2 cups diced cooked lamb
½ cup chopped pecans
2 tablespoons chopped
pimiento

½ cup mayonnaise
¼ cup bottled Italian
dressing
½ teaspoon salt
⅛ teaspoon pepper
Salad greens
Tomato wedges

Cook peas according to package directions. Drain. Stir in
bacon pieces and cool. Toss with lamb, pecans, pimiento,
mayonnaise, Italian dressing, salt, and pepper. Serve on
salad greens; garnish with tomato wedges.

❂

Lamb-Pineapple Luncheon Salad

Makes 4 servings

2 cups cooked diced lamb

1 No. 2 can (1 pound, 4 ounces) pineapple chunks, drained

1½ cups diced celery

½ cup green pepper

1 tablespoon pineapple juice

¾ cup salad dressing

Combine lamb, pineapple, celery, and green pepper. Mix pineapple juice into salad dressing; add to lamb mixture and toss well.

❈

Lamb Chef's Salad

Makes 4 to 6 servings

2 cups diced cooked lamb

2 cups torn lettuce

2 cups torn chicory

1 cup diced Swiss cheese

2 medium-sized tomatoes, cut in wedges

1 medium-sized green pepper, sliced

1 medium-sized red onion, sliced

1 cup grated carrot

⅓ cup salad or olive oil

¼ cup vinegar

1 tablespoon sugar

1 teaspoon paprika

2 tablespoons chopped parsley

2 teaspoons salt

¼ teaspoon pepper

Combine lamb, lettuce, chicory, cheese, tomatoes, green pepper, onion, and carrot; toss lightly. Chill. Combine remaining ingredients; mix well. Pour dressing over lamb mixture. Toss lightly but thoroughly.

❈

Sandwiches

✼✼✼✼✼✼✼ ✼✼✼✼✼✼✼✼ ✼✼✼✼

There are dozens of hot and cold sandwiches which can be made with lamb.

Here are burgers of a wide variety, broiled open-face types, sloppy Joes and ground cooked-lamb spreads.

Not mentioned in the following pages is the cold sandwich made with leftover lamb roast and bread or toast. Leftover lamb roast used for this purpose should be thoroughly chilled.

Lamb-Pickle-Cheese Sandwiches

Makes 4 servings

8 slices rye bread	2 tablespoons chili sauce
¼ cup mayonnaise	½ cup sliced sweet gherkins
4 large slices cooked lamb, about ¼ inch thick	4 slices Swiss cheese

Spread four slices of bread with mayonnaise. Top with lamb, chili sauce, pickles, and cheese. Top with remaining four slices of bread.

❖

Lamb Sloppy Joes

Makes 8 servings

2 pounds ground lamb
1 cup chopped onion
1 cup chopped green pepper
1½ teaspoons salt
¼ teaspoon pepper
1⅓ cups catsup

2 tablespoons prepared mustard
1 cup (about 4 ounces) grated Cheddar cheese
8 hamburger buns, heated
Parsley sprigs

Turn lamb, onion, and green pepper into 10-inch skillet. Cook 15 minutes over medium heat, stirring occasionally. Add salt, pepper, catsup, and mustard; stir. Cook 10 minutes over low heat, stirring occasionally. Add cheese; stir. Cook, stirring frequently, until cheese melts. Serve over buns. Garnish with parsley, as desired.

❁

Western Lamb Chili Burger

Makes 4 servings

1 pound ground lamb
1 can (1 pound) kidney beans, drained
⅓ cup chili sauce

4 crisp lettuce leaves
4 hamburger buns, split, toasted and buttered
Onion slices

Shape lamb into four flat patties. Broil, 3 to 4 inches from source of heat, 5 to 7 minutes on each side. Meanwhile, combine kidney beans and chili sauce; stir. Cook over medium heat to desired degree of doneness. Arrange lettuce, lamb patties, and chili mixture on buns. Serve with onion slices.

❁

Tomato-Cheese Lamburgers

Makes 6 servings

- 1½ pounds ground lamb
- ½ cup fine dry bread crumbs
- 1 egg, beaten
- 1 teaspoon garlic salt
- 6 slices Bermuda onion
- 6 slices tomato
- 6 slices processed Swiss cheese

Combine lamb, bread crumbs, egg, and garlic salt; mix well. Shape into six patties. Broil, 3 to 4 inches from source of heat, or cook on outdoor grill, 4 to 5 minutes. Turn, cook 3 minutes. Top with remaining ingredients. Cook 2 minutes.

❁

Ground Lamb Sandwich

Makes 4 servings

- 1 pound ground lamb
- 1 medium-sized green pepper, chopped
- ¼ cup chopped chives
- 1 can (8 ounces) tomato sauce
- 1 teaspoon salt
- ¼ teaspoon pepper
- 4 slices white toast, buttered

Cook lamb over low heat, stirring occasionally, until browned. Add green pepper and chives and cook 5 minutes. Add tomato sauce, salt, and pepper. Cover and cook 30 minutes, stirring occasionally. Arrange lamb mixture over toast.

❁

Open-Face Lamb Sandwiches

Makes 4 servings

2 tablespoons salad oil
1 pound ground lamb
1 clove garlic, crushed
¼ cup chopped celery
1 medium-sized green
  pepper, sliced

1 teaspoon salt
1 medium-sized onion,
  sliced
3 tablespoons chili sauce
2 hard seeded rolls
Grated Parmesan cheese

Heat oil. Add lamb and garlic and cook until lamb is browned. Drain off drippings if necessary. Add celery, green pepper, salt, onion, and chili sauce. Cover and cook over low heat, stirring occasionally, 15 minutes or until vegetables are tender. Cut rolls in half. Arrange lamb mixture on roll halves. Sprinkle with Parmesan cheese. Broil, 5 inches from source of heat, 2 to 3 minutes.

❈

Lamb and Cheese Sandwiches

Makes 4 servings

4 large slices cooked lamb,
  about ¼ inch thick
4 slices processed
  American cheese

8 slices white bread,
  buttered
1 tablespoon prepared
  mustard
3 tablespoons chili sauce

Arrange lamb and cheese on 4 slices of bread. Spread with mustard and chili sauce. Top with remaining 4 slices of bread.

❈

Skillet Lamburgers with Blue Cheese

Makes 6 servings

1½ pounds ground lamb
¾ cup chopped onion
¼ cup chopped parsley
1 egg, beaten
1 clove garlic, finely chopped
1 teaspoon salt

2 tablespoons shortening
1 can (8 ounces) tomato sauce
1 tablespoon lemon juice
¼ cup (about 1¼ ounces) Blue cheese, crumbled
6 hamburger buns

Combine lamb, ½ cup onion, parsley, egg, garlic, and salt. Mix well and shape into six burgers. Melt shortening; add burgers and cook until browned on both sides.

Meanwhile, combine tomato sauce, remaining ¼ cup onion and lemon juice; heat to boiling point. Add cheese. Serve on lamburgers with buns.

❁

Sherry Lamburgers

Makes 4 servings

1 pound ground lamb
1 cup grated potatoes
¼ cup dry sherry

2 tablespoons orange juice
1 teaspoon salt
⅛ teaspoon pepper

Combine all ingredients; mix well. Shape into four patties. Broil, 3 to 4 inches from source of heat, or cook on outdoor grill 5 to 7 minutes. Turn patties and cook about 5 minutes.

❁

Lamb & Egg Salad Sandwich Spread

Makes about 3 cups

2 cups chopped cooked lamb

4 hard-cooked eggs, chopped

¼ cup chopped canned pimientos

½ cup mayonnaise

1 teaspoon garlic salt

¼ teaspoon pepper

Combine all ingredients; mix well. Spread on buttered bread slices.

❋

Lamb & Minted Onion Sandwiches

Makes 6 to 12 sandwiches

½ teaspoon dehydrated mint leaves

1 tablespoon chopped parsley

¼ teaspoon thyme

Salt and pepper to taste

¼ cup vinegar

½ cup olive or salad oil

3 large sweet Spanish onions, cut in ¼-inch slices

Sliced cooked lamb

Sliced rye bread

Combine mint, parsley, thyme, salt and pepper, vinegar and oil; blend or shake well. Arrange half of onion slices in shallow dish. Pour half of mint mixture over onions, repeat layers using remaining mint mixture and onion slices. Chill 1 hour, spooning some of mint mixture over onions occasionally. Arrange minted onion slices and lamb slices on rye bread.

❋

Ground-Lamb & Olive Nests

Makes 6 servings

> 6 hamburger buns
> 1½ pounds ground lamb
> ⅓ cup chopped pimiento-stuffed green olives
> ½ cup mayonnaise

> ¼ teaspoon pepper
> 4 slices mozzarella cheese, about ¼ inch thick
> Sliced pimiento-stuffed green olives

Hollow out centers of buns, leaving ½-inch shell. Crumble bread removed from centers. Combine crumbled bread, lamb, chopped olives, mayonnaise, and pepper; mix well. Press lamb mixture firmly into bun shells. Cut each slice of cheese into three strips. Top lamb mixture with cheese. Arrange on baking sheet. Bake in oven at 425° for 15 minutes. Garnish with olive slices. Serve with mustard and catsup, if desired.

❂

Open Hero Sandwiches

Makes 4 servings

> 2 small loaves French bread, halved
> 2 tablespoons prepared garlic spread
> 4 slices imported Swiss cheese

> 8 slices (about ¼ inch thick) cooked lamb leg or shoulder
> 4 canned pimientos
> 1 dill pickle, sliced

Spread bread with garlic spread. Arrange remaining ingredients on bread.

❂

Lamb Chili Sandwiches

Makes 4 servings

1 pound ground lamb
1 medium-sized onion,
, chopped
1 can (8 ounces) tomato
sauce

½ cup chili sauce
Salt and pepper to taste
4 slices bread, toasted

Cook lamb over low heat until browned, stirring occasionally. Add onion and cook 5 minutes. Add tomato sauce, chili sauce, and salt and pepper; mix well. Cover and cook 20 minutes, stirring occasionally. Serve lamb-chili mixture over toast.

❁

Lamb Cheeseburgers

Makes 4 servings

1 pound ground lamb
½ cup corn flakes
1 egg
1 teaspoon salt
¼ teaspoon pepper
¼ teaspoon thyme

1 tablespoon dehydrated
minced onion
4 slices processed
American cheese
4 hamburger buns, split,
toasted, and buttered

Combine lamb, corn flakes, egg, salt, pepper, thyme, and onion; mix well. Shape into four patties. Broil, 3 to 4 inches from source of heat, or cook on outdoor grill 5 to 7 minutes. Turn and cook 5 to 7 minutes or until desired degree of doneness. Top with cheese and broil 1 to 2 minutes or until cheese melts. Serve on buns.

❁

Lamburgers & Beans

Makes 6 servings

1½ pounds ground lamb
⅓ cup shredded radish
1 teaspoon salt
¼ teaspoon pepper
½ teaspoon Tabasco

1 can (1 pound) pork and
beans
1 teaspoon chili powder
6 hamburger buns,
toasted, buttered

Combine lamb, radish, salt, pepper, and Tabasco; mix well. Shape into six patties. Broil, 4 to 5 inches from source of heat, 4 to 5 minutes; turn and broil 2 to 3 minutes.

Meanwhile, combine beans and chili powder. Arrange beans on lamburgers and broil 2 to 3 minutes. Serve on buns.

❖

Broiled Bacon Lamburgers

Makes 4 servings

1 pound ground lamb
½ teaspoon salt
¼ teaspoon cinnamon
⅛ teaspoon cloves

⅛ teaspoon allspice
8 slices bacon
4 English muffins, split,
toasted, and buttered

Combine lamb, salt, cinnamon, cloves, and allspice; mix well. Shape into four patties. Wrap each patty with two slices bacon. Broil, 3 to 4 inches from source of heat, or cook on outdoor grill, 5 minutes on each side. Serve on muffin halves.

❖

Lamb Cucumber Hero

Makes 4 servings

14-inch loaf Italian bread, split and buttered	Sliced cooked lamb
Lettuce	Marinated cucumber slices (see below)
4 or 5 thin slices red or sweet onion	Miniature dill pickles and pimiento-stuffed olives
4 slices Muenster cheese	Mayonnaise or mustard

Layer on bottom half of bread the lettuce, onion, cheese, lamb, and 1 cup drained marinated cucumber slices. Cover with top half of bread; secure with picks, garnish with pickles and olives. Serve with remaining cucumber and mayonnaise or mustard, as desired.

Marinated Cucumber Slices

Combine 1 medium cucumber, thinly sliced, with 3 tablespoons each of salad oil and vinegar, ½ teaspoon salt, ¼ teaspoon dill seed; and dash each of pepper and garlic powder, or use ½ cup bottled Italian dressing. Chill about 8 hours, turning cucumber slices once.

❉

Tasty Lamb Sandwiches

Makes 4 servings

2 cups finely chopped cooked lamb	⅓ cup chili sauce
½ cup chopped celery	½ teaspoon salt
⅓ cup chopped parsley	¼ teaspoon pepper
1 tablespoon dehydrated minced onion	8 slices bread, buttered

Combine lamb, celery, parsley, onion, chili sauce, salt, and pepper; mix well. Chill. Spread on bread to make sandwiches.

❉

Barbecued Lamb Sandwiches

Makes 4 servings

¼ cup French dressing
½ cup chili sauce
½ cup firmly packed light-brown sugar

8 slices cooked lamb
4 slices bread

Combine French dressing, chili sauce and light-brown sugar; mix well. Arrange eight slices cooked lamb on four slices bread. Top with French-dressing mixture. Broil, 3 to 4 inches from source of heat, 5 to 7 minutes.

❉

Chutney Lamb Patties

Makes 4 servings

1 pound ground lamb
1 small onion, chopped
¾ teaspoon celery salt
¼ teaspoon pepper

⅓ cup chutney
4 hamburger buns, split in half and toasted

Combine lamb, onion, celery salt, pepper, and chutney; mix well. Shape into four patties. Broil, 3 to 4 inches from source of heat, 5 to 7 minutes. Turn and broil 5 minutes or until lamb is desired degree of doneness. Serve chutney lamb patties on buns.

❉

Curry Lamb Patties

Makes 6 servings

1 pound ground lamb
1 cup cooked rice
1/3 cup chopped almonds
1/2 cup finely chopped onion
1 tablespoon curry powder

1 teaspoon salt
1/4 teaspoon pepper
1 egg, beaten
6 hamburger buns, split and toasted

Combine lamb, rice, almonds, onion, curry powder, salt, pepper, and egg; mix well. Shape into six patties. Broil, 3 to 4 inches from source of heat, 5 to 6 minutes. Turn patties and broil 5 to 6 minutes or until well done. Serve on buns.

❖

Diced or Cubed Lamb

❧❧❧❧❧❧❧❧ ❧❧ ❧❧❧❧❧❧❧❧ ❧❧ ❧❧❧❧

For Stews, Pies, and Casseroles

Who says that a stew has to be uninteresting? There are as many kinds of stew as there are people with imaginations. Every nation has its own distinctive kind of stew or stews. In the following pages you'll find recipes for American, Irish, Scotch, Italian, French, Spanish, and Near Eastern types. Every one will provide a treat.

The same holds true for the casseroles and pies described, which range from lamb curry to lamb Tetrazzini, shepherd's pie, lamb Stroganoff, pilaff, and paprikash!

In many of the following dishes, "bone-in" cuts (riblets or neck meat) may be used instead of the cubes called for.

Autumn Lamb Stew

Makes 6 servings

2 tablespoons butter
1½ pounds diced lamb shoulder
1 medium-sized onion, sliced
½ cup chopped celery
1 small clove garlic, crushed
1 medium-sized green pepper, chopped

2 cups stock or bouillon
6 small potatoes, pared and quartered
4 small carrots, diced
1 cup diced eggplant
1½ teaspoons salt
¼ teaspoon pepper
¼ cup all-purpose flour
½ cup water

Melt butter; add lamb and cook over low heat, stirring occasionally, until browned on all sides. Add onion, celery, garlic, and green pepper and cook 5 minutes. Add stock or bouillon. Cover and cook 30 minutes. Add potatoes and cook 10 minutes. Add carrots, eggplant, salt, and pepper and cook, covered, 10 minutes, or until vegetables are tender. Remove lamb and vegetables. Combine flour and water; blend. Add flour mixture to stock or bouillon mixture; blend. Cook over low heat, stirring constantly, until thickened. Add vegetables and lamb to stock or bouillon mixture.

❖

American Lamb Stew

Makes 6 servings

2 tablespoons shortening
1½ pounds lamb shoulder, cubed
1 cup sliced onion
1 can (1 pound) whole baby carrots, drained
1 can (1 pound) green peas, drained
1 can (1 pound, 12 ounces) tomatoes
1 cup sliced mushrooms
1 envelope onion-soup mix (1½ ounces)
2 cups flour, sifted
3 teaspoons baking powder
1 teaspoon salt
1 tablespoon caraway seed
⅓ cup salad oil
⅔ cup milk

Melt shortening. Brown lamb and onion in skillet over low heat. Add carrots, peas, tomatoes, mushrooms, and onion-soup mix; stir well. Drain off excess fat, if any. Turn into 3-quart casserole. Cover and bake in oven at 350° for 1 hour or until lamb is tender.

Sift together flour, baking powder, and salt; stir in caraway seed. Measure oil, then milk, into 1-cup measure (don't stir together). Pour over flour mixture; mix until dough cleans sides of bowl. Knead dough 10 times or until smooth. Roll to ¼- to ½-inch thickness. Cut with biscuit cutter. Place on top of stew; bake in oven at 450° for 10 to 15 minutes or until biscuits are golden brown.

❈

Easy Brown Lamb Stew

Makes 4 servings

1½ pounds boneless lamb
shoulder, diced
Seasoned flour
2 tablespoons salad oil
2 cloves garlic, finely
chopped

2 cups water
1 package (10 ounces)
frozen mixed vegetables
Salt and pepper to taste
½ teaspoon rosemary

Coat lamb with seasoned flour. Heat oil; add lamb and cook until lightly browned on all sides. Add garlic and water. Cover and cook 1 hour over low heat, stirring occasionally. Add remaining ingredients. Cover and cook 10 minutes or until vegetables are tender, stirring occasionally.

❊

Lamb Stew with Parsley Dumplings

Makes 6 servings

1 tablespoon shortening
1½ pounds lamb shoulder,
cubed
1 cup small white onions
3 medium-sized carrots,
quartered
1 can (6 ounces) whole
mushrooms, drained
(optional)

1 quart stock or bouillon
1½ teaspoons salt
¼ teaspoon pepper
1 teaspoon garlic salt
2 cups biscuit mix
¼ cup chopped parsley
¾ cup milk

Melt shortening in kettle. Add lamb and cook over low heat until browned on all sides. Add onions, carrots, mushrooms, stock or bouillon, salt, pepper, and garlic salt. Cover and cook over low heat about 45 minutes or until lamb is tender. Combine remaining ingredients; stir lightly. Drop by tablespoonfuls into lamb mixture. Cover and cook about 10 minutes or until dumplings are done.

❁

Lamb Stew with Parmesan Croutons

Makes 6 servings

1 tablespoon shortening	¼ teaspoon pepper
1½ pounds lamb shoulder, cubed	3 tablespoons all-purpose flour
½ cup sliced onion	¼ cup chopped canned pimientos
2 cups stock or bouillon	¼ cup melted butter
1 medium-sized head cauliflower, broken into florets	½ cup grated Parmesan cheese
2 cups diced tomatoes	2 cups ½-inch bread cubes
1½ teaspoons salt	

Melt shortening in kettle. Add lamb and onion. Cook over low heat until lamb is browned on all sides. Add stock or bouillon. Cover and cook 30 minutes over low heat. Add cauliflower, tomatoes, salt, and pepper. Cover and cook 30 minutes over low heat or until lamb and vegetables are tender, stirring occasionally. Add a little of lamb liquid to flour; blend. Add to lamb mixture with pimientos. Cook until slightly thickened, stirring constantly.

Meanwhile, combine remaining ingredients; mix well. Broil 3 to 4 inches from source of heat 2 to 3 minutes or until lightly browned. Serve stew topped with croutons.

❁

Highland Lamb Stew

Makes 6 servings

2½ pounds lamb shoulder, cubed
2 tablespoons salad oil
1 teaspoon salt
1 teaspoon nutmeg
½ teaspoon crushed thyme
1¼ cups water
2 medium-sized onions, sliced

1 clove garlic, crushed
1 package (1⅜ ounces) sour-cream-sauce mix
1 can (10¾ ounces) condensed Scotch broth
1 medium-sized head cabbage, cut in 6 wedges, cooked

Brown lamb in hot oil in skillet over medium heat, stirring occasionally. Add seasonings, water, onions, and garlic. Stir well; cover and cook over low heat 50 to 60 minutes or until tender. In small bowl, blend sour-cream-sauce mix with Scotch broth; stir into lamb and cook over low heat 10 minutes longer. Arrange hot cabbage in heated serving dish and pour lamb stew over top.

❁

Light Irish Lamb Stew

Makes 6 servings

2 pounds lamb shoulder, cubed
2½ teaspoons salt
¼ teaspoon pepper
1 teaspoon monosodium glutamate
2 or 3 bay leaves

Water
4½ cups diced potatoes
2 cups sliced carrots
2 cups sliced onions
¾ cup drained canned or cooked peas

Combine lamb, salt, pepper, monosodium glutamate, bay leaves, and enough water to cover. Heat to boiling point. Cover and cook over low heat 30 minutes. Chill. Skim off fat from surface. Add potatoes, carrots, and onions to lamb mixture. Cover and cook 45 minutes over low heat or until lamb and vegetables are tender. Add peas. Cook 5 minutes.

❁

Succotash Lamb Stew

Makes 4 to 6 servings

2 tablespoons butter
1 pound diced shoulder of lamb
1 medium-sized onion, chopped
1 clove garlic, chopped
4 medium-sized tomatoes, diced
½ cup stock or bouillon
1½ teaspoons salt

¼ teaspoon pepper
3 tablespoons all-purpose flour
3 tablespoons water
1 package (10 ounces) frozen cut corn
1½ cups cooked lima beans
Cooked rice

Melt butter; add lamb, onion, and garlic and cook over medium heat until lamb is browned, stirring occasionally. Add tomatoes, stock or bouillon, salt and pepper; mix well. Cover and cook 40 minutes over low heat, stirring occasionally. Blend flour with water. Add flour mixture, corn, and beans to lamb mixture; mix well. Cover and cook 10 minutes over low heat, stirring occasionally. Serve with rice.

❁

Halloween Lamb Stew

Makes 4 servings

2 tablespoons salad oil
1 pound lamb shoulder, diced
1 cup sliced celery
1 can (1 pound) whole white onions, drained
1 can (1 pound) tomatoes
1 cup sliced carrots
1 teaspoon celery salt
1/8 teaspoon pepper
2 tablespoons all-purpose flour
1/4 cup water

Heat oil; add lamb and cook until browned on all sides. Add celery and cook 5 minutes. Add onions and undrained tomatoes. Cover and cook 20 minutes. Add carrots, celery salt, and pepper. Cover and cook 20 minutes or until lamb is tender. Combine flour and water; blend. Slowly stir flour mixture into lamb mixture and cook over low heat, stirring constantly, until thickened. Serve topped with pastry cut-outs, if desired.

❈

Lamb Cranberry Stew

Makes 4 servings

1 pound shoulder of lamb, diced
1 teaspoon seasoned salt
2 tablespoons butter
2 1/4 cups stock or bouillon
1 cup bottled cranberry-juice cocktail
1/3 cup cornstarch
1/2 cup water
1 teaspoon salt
1 can (1 pound) whole carrots, drained
1 package (10 ounces) French-cut green beans, thawed

Sprinkle lamb with seasoned salt. Melt butter; add lamb and cook over medium heat until lamb is browned on all sides. Add stock or bouillon and cranberry-juice cocktail. Cover and cook over low heat about 2 hours or until lamb is tender. Combine cornstarch and water; mix well. Gradually add cornstarch mixture to lamb mixture and cook over low heat, stirring constantly, until thickened. Add salt, carrots, and beans. Cook over low heat, stirring occasionally, for 10 minutes or until beans are tender.

❁

Mexican Lamb-Pinto Stew

Makes 6 servings

2 pounds lamb shoulder, cubed
¼ cup flour
3 tablespoons salad oil
1 medium-sized onion, sliced
1 cup stock or bouillon
1½ cups cooked pinto beans
1 can (12 ounces) whole-kernel corn, undrained
1 jar (4 ounces) pimientos, drained and chopped
1 medium-sized green pepper, cut in strips
1 teaspoon salt
½ teaspoon pepper
½ teaspoon basil
½ teaspoon thyme

Coat lamb with flour. In large skillet, brown lamb on all sides in hot oil. Remove lamb; add onion to skillet and cook until golden. Stir in remaining ingredients, then lamb; turn into lightly greased 2-quart casserole. Cover and bake in oven at 350° for 1 hour or until lamb is tender.

❁

Near Eastern Stew

Makes 6 servings

4 artichokes
¼ cup flour
2 teaspoons salt
¼ teaspoon turmeric
½ teaspoon oregano
2 pounds lamb shoulder, boned and cubed

2 tablespoons salad oil
1 can (1 pound) whole carrots
6 medium-sized onions, whole or cut in half
1 tablespoon lemon juice

Wash artichokes; trim stems and pull off tough outer leaves. Cut artichokes in quarters; remove chokes (fuzzy portion). Mix flour and seasonings; add lamb and toss until well coated. Brown lamb in hot oil in skillet. Drain liquid from carrots and add water to make 3½ cups; stir liquid into skillet. Cook and stir until mixture thickens slightly; add onions. Cover and simmer 30 minutes, stirring if needed. Arrange artichokes on top of lamb; cover and cook slowly 20 minutes. Mix in lemon juice. Add carrots and heat. Serve with hot cooked rice if desired.

❈

Baked Lamb Stew
with Cornmeal Biscuits

Makes 6 servings

1 tablespoon shortening
1½ pounds lamb shoulder, cubed
1 cup sliced onion
1½ cups sliced beets
1½ cups cut green beans
2 cups diced tomatoes

1 cup sliced mushrooms (optional)
3 cups stock or bouillon
Salt and pepper to taste
1½ cups biscuit mix
½ cup yellow cornmeal
½ cup milk

Melt shortening in skillet. Add lamb and onion. Cook over low heat until lamb is browned on all sides. Add beets, beans, tomatoes, mushrooms, stock or bouillon, and salt and pepper; mix well. Turn into 3-quart casserole. Cover and bake in oven at 350° for 1 hour or until lamb is tender. Combine biscuit mix and cornmeal. Add milk and mix lightly. Turn out on lightly floured surface and knead gently 10 times. Roll out to ½-inch thickness. Cut into 2½-inch rounds, using floured cutter. Arrange biscuits over stew. Bake in oven at 400° for about 15 minutes or until biscuits are done.

❊

Brown Irish Lamb Stew

Makes 6 servings

1 tablespoon shortening	2 cups stock or bouillon
1½ pounds lamb shoulder, cubed	3 cups sliced potatoes
	2 cups diced turnips
1½ teaspoons salt	2 cups sliced carrots
½ teaspoon pepper	1 cup sliced onions
½ teaspoon sage	1 cup cut green beans
¼ teaspoon celery seed	

Melt shortening in kettle. Combine lamb, salt, pepper, sage, and celery seed. Cook over low heat until lamb is browned on all sides. Add stock or bouillon. Cover and cook 30 minutes over low heat. Add remaining ingredients. Cover and cook over low heat about 30 to 45 minutes or until vegetables are tender, stirring occasionally.

❊

Sancocho Lamb Stew

Makes 10 servings

2 pounds lamb shoulder, diced

1 medium-sized onion, sliced

1 medium-sized tomato, cut in wedges

1 medium-sized green pepper, sliced

¼ teaspoon coriander seed

3 quarts water

1 can (8 ounces) whole-kernel corn, drained

2½ cups (1 pound) pared and chopped white potatoes

4 cups (1½ pounds) pared and chopped yams

1 green banana, peeled and chopped

1 can (8 ounces) tomato sauce

2 ripe bananas, peeled and chopped

1 cup sifted all-purpose flour

Salt and pepper to taste

Combine lamb, onion, tomato, green pepper, coriander seed, and water. Heat to boiling. Reduce heat; cover and cook 30 minutes. Remove vegetables. Force vegetables through sieve or food mill. Combine sieved vegetables, corn, potatoes, yams, green banana, tomato sauce, and ripe banana with lamb mixture. Stir to blend. Cover and cook over low heat for 45 minutes or until vegetables are tender. Combine flour, salt, and pepper; blend. Remove 2 cups liquid from stew. Slowly stir into flour mixture until smooth. Stir flour mixture into stew. Cook over low heat, stirring constantly, until stew is thickened.

Lamb Stew with Celery in Avgolemono Sauce

Makes 6 servings

2 pounds lamb, cut in
chunks
1 large onion, chopped
¼ cup oil
Salt and pepper to taste

1 cup water (about)
1 large bunch celery
Avgolemono sauce (see
below)

Brown meat and onions in oil. Season and add water.
Cook over medium heat until meat is partially done. Add
celery, cut in 2-inch pieces. When celery and meat are
done, place on platter; make Avgolemono sauce to pour
over all. Stew may be served over rice.

Avgolemono Sauce I

4 eggs
Juice of 1½ lemons

Pan drippings (about 2
cups) from pan in which
lamb was cooked

Beat eggs until frothy; add lemon juice slowly, beating
constantly. Then add liquid from pan slowly, beating
constantly, until it becomes slightly thickened.

❀

Lamb Paprika

Makes 6 servings

3 tablespoons shortening
1 clove garlic, finely chopped
2 medium-sized onions, sliced
2 pounds lamb shoulder, diced
2 tablespoons chopped parsley

1 small green pepper, sliced
2 teaspoons salt
¼ teaspoon pepper
2 tablespoons paprika
2 cups water
2 tablespoons cornstarch
2 tablespoons water

Melt shortening; add garlic, onions, and lamb, and cook until lamb is lightly browned on all sides. Add parsley, green pepper, seasonings, and 2 cups water. Cover and cook over low heat 1 hour or until lamb is tender. Combine cornstarch and 2 tablespoons water; blend. Add to lamb mixture and cook until thickened and clear, stirring constantly.

❁

George Washington Lamb Pie

Makes 4 to 6 servings

2 tablespoons salad oil
1 pound lamb shoulder, diced
1 can (17 ounces) dark sweet pitted cherries
¼ cup blanched almonds

3 tablespoons flour
1 teaspoon salt
½ teaspoon crushed mint leaves
Plain pastry for a two-crust pie

Heat oil; add lamb and cook over low heat until browned on all sides. Remove lamb; reserve drippings. Drain cherries and add enough water to cherry syrup to make one cup liquid. Combine cherries, lamb, and almonds. Add flour to drippings; blend. Add cherry-syrup mixture to flour and cook over low heat, stirring constantly, until thickened. Stir in salt and mint leaves. Add to lamb mixture.

Divide pastry in half. Roll out half of pastry on lightly floured surface to fit 9-inch pie plate. Line pie plate with pastry. Turn lamb mixture into shell. Roll remaining dough to form top crust. Adjust top pastry crust. Trim and flute edges. Cut several slits in top crust. Bake in oven at 425° for 35 to 40 minutes.

❄

Lamb Pie

Makes 4 servings

1 tablespoon oil
1 pound lamb shoulder, diced
2 medium-sized onions, sliced
½ cup chopped celery
⅓ cup chopped canned pimientos

1 can (10½ ounces) condensed cream of celery soup
¾ teaspoon salt
⅛ teaspoon pepper
1 unbaked 9-inch pastry shell

Cook lamb in oil over low heat until browned on all sides. Add onions and celery and cook 5 minutes. Add pimientos, condensed soup, salt, and pepper; mix well. Turn into pastry shell. Bake in oven at 375° for 30 to 40 minutes.

❄

Lamb Stroganoff I

Makes 8 servings

2 pounds boneless lamb
shoulder, cut into 1½
inch strips
Seasoned flour
¼ cup butter
1 clove garlic, mashed
1 cup chopped onion
1 pound mushrooms,
sliced

1 can (10½ ounces)
condensed cream of
celery soup
1½ cups water
Salt and pepper to taste
2 cups commercial sour
cream
Chopped fresh dill
Cooked rice

Coat lamb with flour. Melt butter; add lamb and cook
until browned on all sides. Add garlic, onion, and
mushrooms. Cook 10 minutes over low heat, stirring
occasionally. Add soup, water, and salt and pepper. Cover
and cook 15 minutes over low heat, stirring occasionally.
Stir in sour cream and heat through over low heat. Sprinkle
with dill. Serve with rice.

❂

Lamb Stroganoff II

Makes 6 servings

1½ pounds boneless lamb
shoulder, thinly sliced
Seasoned flour
⅓ cup butter
1 clove garlic, finely
chopped
½ cup chopped onion

1 pound mushrooms,
sliced
Salt and pepper to taste
1½ cups commercial sour
cream
3 tablespoons dry sherry
(optional)

Coat lamb with flour. Melt butter; add lamb, garlic, and
onion and cook until lamb is lightly browned on all sides.
Add mushrooms and salt and pepper. Cover and cook
20 minutes over low heat, stirring occasionally. Add sour
cream and sherry and mix well. Serve with cooked rice,
if desired.

❁

Lamb Paprikash

Makes 8 servings

3 pounds lamb shoulder,
  cut into 1-inch cubes
3 tablespoons salad oil
1 tablespoon salt
½ teaspoon freshly ground
  black pepper
3 tablespoons paprika
2 medium-sized onions,
  thinly sliced

1 cup hot water
2 cups commercial sour
  cream
1 pound medium egg
  noodles
1 cup slivered blanched
  almonds
1 tablespoon poppy seed

Brown lamb well in hot oil; drain off drippings. Sprinkle
with salt, pepper, and paprika. Add onions and water;
cover and simmer 45 minutes or until lamb is tender,
stirring occasionally. Gradually stir in sour cream; heat
but do not boil.

Meanwhile, cook noodles according to package directions;
drain in colander. Toss with almonds and poppy seed;
arrange on serving platter; pour lamb with sauce over
noodles.

❁

Italian Lamb Casserole

Makes 4 servings

2 tablespoons olive or salad oil
1 pound lamb shoulder, diced
1 medium-sized onion, sliced
1 tablespoon salt
3 quarts boiling water
2 cups (8 ounces) elbow macaroni
1 can (1 pound, 13 ounces) tomatoes

1 clove garlic, crushed
½ teaspoon basil
½ teaspoon oregano
2 teaspoons salt
1 teaspoon sugar
⅛ teaspoon pepper
1 package (8 ounces) mozzarella cheese, sliced

Heat oil; add lamb and onion and cook until lamb is browned on all sides. Drain off drippings if necessary.

Meanwhile, add 1 tablespoon salt to rapidly boiling water. Gradually add macaroni so that water continues to boil. Cook uncovered, stirring occasionally, until tender. Drain in colander.

Combine undrained tomatoes, macaroni, garlic, basil, oregano, 2 teaspoons salt, sugar, pepper, and lamb mixture. Turn into 2-quart casserole. Top with cheese. Bake in oven at 350° for 30 minutes. Broil, 5 to 7 inches from source of heat, 3 to 5 minutes or until cheese is browned.

❊

Neapolitan Lamb Risotto

Makes 6 servings

2 tablespoons butter
1 clove garlic
2 pounds lamb shoulder, cut into 1-inch cubes
1 medium-sized onion, chopped
2 tablespoons catsup

1 teaspoon salt
½ teaspoon Tabasco
1 cup water
1 cup bouillon
1 cup uncooked rice
¼ cup grated Parmesan cheese

Melt butter in large skillet. Add garlic and lamb; cook over medium heat until lamb is browned on all sides. Remove garlic. Add onion and continue cooking until onion is tender. Stir in catsup, salt, Tabasco, water, and bouillon; bring to a boil. Cover and cook over very low heat for 1 hour or until lamb is tender. Remove lamb. Measure sauce and add water to make 3 cups; return sauce to skillet; bring to a boil. Add rice; cover and cook 20 to 25 minutes or until rice is tender. Add lamb and Parmesan cheese; heat through.

❊

Lamb Hot Pot

Makes 6 servings

1½ pounds lamb shoulder, cubed	2 cups diced potatoes
1½ teaspoons salt	1 cup sliced carrots
½ teaspoon pepper	1 cup sliced onion
1 cup stock or bouillon	1 cup cut corn

Salt and pepper lamb; cook over low heat until lamb is browned on all sides. Add remaining ingredients. Turn into 2½-quart casserole. Cover and bake in oven at 350° for 1 hour or until lamb and vegetables are tender.

❁

Lamb Hash with Poached Eggs

Makes 4 servings

2 tablespoons salad oil	2 cups diced potatoes
1 pound fresh or cooked lamb shoulder, diced	1 teaspoon salt
¾ cup chopped onion	¼ teaspoon pepper
	4 poached eggs

Heat oil; add lamb and cook over low heat until browned on all sides. Add onion and potatoes and cook 10 minutes. Add salt and pepper. Cover and cook 20 minutes, stirring occasionally. Serve lamb hash topped with eggs.

❁

Persian Lamb Skillet

Makes 6 servings

2½ pounds boned lamb
shoulder, cubed
2 tablespoons salad oil
½ teaspoon salt
¼ teaspoon pepper
½ teaspoon turmeric
¼ teaspoon cinnamon
1 can (1 pound) small
whole onions

1 teaspoon white vinegar
1 cup water
2 tablespoons cornstarch
1 can (1 pound) kidney
beans, drained
Cooked rice
Parsley

Brown lamb in oil in skillet over medium heat, stirring
occasionally. Mix together salt, pepper, turmeric, and
cinnamon; sprinkle over browned lamb. Drain onions,
reserving liquid. Pour onion liquid, vinegar, and ¾ cup
of the water over lamb; cover and simmer 50 to 60
minutes or until tender. Mix remaining ¼ cup water with
cornstarch; stir into skillet; cook and stir until thickened.
Add onions and kidney beans and cook 5 minutes longer
or until vegetables are heated through. Serve with rice;
garnish with parsley.

❀

Potato-Lamb-and-Egg Casserole

Makes 4 to 6 servings

1 tablespoon oil
1 pound lamb shoulder, diced
5 medium-sized potatoes peeled, cooked and diced
6 small white onions, quartered
5 hard-cooked eggs, quartered

¼ teaspoon salt
⅛ teaspoon pepper
1 can (10½ ounces) condensed cream of mushroom soup
1⅓ cups water
¼ cup fine dry bread crumbs

Heat oil; add lamb and cook until browned on all sides. Combine lamb, potatoes, onions, eggs, salt, and pepper in greased 2-quart casserole. Blend soup with water. Pour soup over lamb mixture. Top with bread crumbs. Bake in oven at 350° for 25 minutes.

❁

Lamb Pilaff

Makes 6 to 8 servings

1½ teaspoons salt
¼ teaspoon pepper
3 tablespoons lemon juice
3 pounds lamb shoulder, cubed
¼ cup butter
3 cups boiling water

4 teaspoons canned tomato paste
2 cups water
¾ teaspoon cinnamon
3 tablespoons butter
2 cups rice
½ cup pignolia nuts, lightly browned in butter

Combine salt, pepper, and lemon juice. Dip lamb in lemon mixture. Melt ¼ cup butter; add lamb (without lemon mixture) and cook over medium heat until lamb is browned on all sides. Add boiling water. Combine tomato paste, 2 cups water, and cinnamon; blend. Add tomato mixture to lamb. Cover and cook over medium heat 1½ hours. Drain lamb and reserve liquid. Melt 3 tablespoons butter; add rice and cook over medium heat 5 to 6 minutes or until rice is very lightly browned, stirring occasionally. Add lamb liquid; mix well. Cover and cook over medium heat 25 minutes, stirring occasionally. Add lamb and pignolia nuts; heat through.

❁

Ek-Our-Korma (Lamb Curry)

Makes 6 servings

1 tablespoon shortening	2 teaspoons curry powder
1½ pounds lamb shoulder, diced	¼ teaspoon ginger
1 cup sliced onion	1 teaspoon salt
3 tablespoons all-purpose flour	¼ teaspoon pepper
1 tablespoon mint-flavored jelly	1½ cups stock or bouillon
	2 cups hot cooked rice

Melt shortening; add lamb and onion and cook over medium heat until lamb is browned on all sides. Add flour, mint jelly, curry powder, ginger, salt and pepper, and the stock or bouillon. Cover and cook over medium heat 1½ hours or until tender, stirring occasionally. Serve with rice. Serve with chopped toasted almonds and/or salted almonds, chutney, sieved egg yolk, and kumquats, as desired.

❁

Mock Couscous (Moroccan Lamb Stew)

Makes 8 servings

2 tablespoons salad oil
2 pounds lamb shoulder, diced
1 medium-sized onion, chopped
4 cups water
1 bay leaf, crumbled
¼ teaspoon ginger
2½ teaspoons salt
½ teaspoon cumin seed
⅛ teaspoon pepper

2 cups cubed yellow turnip (2-inch cubes)
1 cup sliced carrot
2½ cups sliced zucchini (about 2 medium-sized zucchini)
½ cup seedless raisins
¼ cup all-purpose flour
8 cups hot cooked rice
⅓ cup melted butter
1 tablespoon sugar

Heat oil; add lamb and cook over low heat until browned on all sides. Add onion and cook 5 minutes. Drain off drippings if necessary. Add 3 cups water, bay leaf, ginger, salt, cumin seed, and pepper. Cover and cook 15 minutes. Add turnip and cook, covered, 20 minutes. Add carrots, zucchini, and raisins. Cover and cook over low heat for 10 minutes or until vegetables and lamb are tender. Combine remaining 1 cup water and flour; blend. Gradually add flour mixture to lamb mixture and cook over low heat, stirring constantly, until slightly thickened.

Meanwhile, combine remaining ingredients; mix lightly. Serve lamb stew with rice mixture.

❖

Lamb Tips

Makes 4 servings

2 tablespoons salad oil
1 pound lamb shoulder, diced
1 small onion, chopped
1 cup hot water
1½ teaspoons dry mustard
⅛ teaspoon monosodium glutamate
1 teaspoon salt
½ teaspoon seasoned salt
⅛ teaspoon pepper
1 tablespoon Worcestershire sauce
1 tablespoon brown sugar
½ cup cold water
2 tablespoons all-purpose flour
2 tablespoons chopped pecans
½ cup seedless green grapes
2 cups hot cooked rice

Heat oil in skillet; add lamb and cook until lightly browned on all sides. Add onion and brown lightly. Mix hot water, mustard, monosodium glutamate, salt, seasoned salt, pepper, Worcestershire sauce, and sugar; add to lamb and mix thoroughly. Cover and cook over low heat 30 minutes or until lamb is tender. Gradually stir cold water into flour; blend well. Stir flour mixture into lamb mixture. Cook, stirring constantly, 5 minutes or until thickened. Combine pecans, grapes, and rice; mix lightly. Serve lamb and gravy with rice.

❁

Birayni

Makes 6 servings

3 cloves garlic
1 tablespoon chopped parsley
2 canned green chilies, chopped
1 teaspoon poppy seed
1 teaspoon chopped fresh mint or ¼ teaspoon dry mint flakes
½ teaspoon ginger
¼ teaspoon cinnamon
4 whole cloves
3 tablespoons and 2 cups water

3 tablespoons salad oil
2 pounds boneless lamb shoulder, cut into 1-inch cubes
3 whole cardamom
1 cinnamon stick
¼ cup butter
1½ cups yogurt
1 tablespoon salt
1 pound uncooked rice
⅛ teaspoon saffron
1 teaspoon rose water (optional)

Combine garlic, parsley, chilies, poppy seed, mint, ginger, cinnamon, 2 cloves, 3 tablespoons water, and 1 tablespoon oil and blend in electric blender (or grind dry ingredients; mix with water and oil). Pour over lamb cubes; let stand 2 hours.

Brown cardamom, remaining 2 cloves, and cinnamon stick in heated butter. Mix in lamb and sauce, and yogurt and salt. Cover and simmer 1 hour, 15 minutes, stirring occasionally.

Meanwhile, lightly brown rice in heated 2 tablespoons oil, stirring frequently. Stir in 2 cups water and saffron. Cover and cook about 10 minutes over low heat until water is absorbed. Gently stir rice mixture and rose water into lamb. Cover and cook 15 minutes longer or until lamb is fork-tender. If desired, serve with browned onion rings, toasted almonds, and raisins.

❄

Calcutta Lamb & Coconut Curry on Thin Noodles

Makes 4 servings

¼ cup butter
1 pound lamb shoulder, cubed
1 medium-sized onion, sliced
¼ cup all-purpose flour
½ teaspoon ginger
1 teaspoon salt
1½ tablespoons curry powder (or to taste)
1½ cups stock or bouillon

⅓ cup maraschino cherry juice
¼ cup lemon juice
⅓ cup flaked coconut
⅓ cup light (sultana) seedless raisins
1 tablespoon salt
3 quarts boiling water
8 ounces (about 4 cups) fine egg noodles
Maraschino cherries for garnish

Melt butter; add lamb and onion, and cook over low heat until lamb is browned on all sides. Add flour, ginger, 1 teaspoon salt, and curry powder; blend. Add stock or bouillon, cherry juice, and lemon juice and cook over low heat, stirring constantly, until thickened. Add coconut and raisins; mix. Cover and cook 40 minutes over low heat, stirring occasionally.

Meanwhile, add 1 tablespoon salt to rapidly boiling water. Gradually add noodles so that water continues to boil. Cook uncovered, stirring occasionally, until tender. Drain in colander. Serve curry sauce over noodles. Garnish with maraschino cherries.

❖

Rogan Jaush

Makes 8 servings

6 medium-sized onions, finely chopped
5 tablespoons butter
2 pounds lamb shoulder, cut into 3-inch cubes
1½ tablespoons coriander
¾ tablespoon turmeric
½ tablespoon cumin
¾ teaspoon ginger
¼ teaspoon red chili
Salt to taste
6 tablespoons yogurt
¼ cup seedless raisins
½ cup chopped apple
3 tomatoes, chopped
½ cup water

Cook onions in the butter until well browned. Add lamb, coriander, turmeric, cumin, and ginger. Cook over low heat, stirring constantly, for 12 minutes. Add chili, salt, yogurt, raisins, apple, and tomatoes; mix well. Cook until all the moisture has been absorbed. Add water. Cover and cook until water is reduced. Repeat, adding water and reducing, until meat is tender.

❋

Bildocha Irrisaikin (Lamb with Rice)

Makes 6 to 8 servings

1 tablespoon olive oil or other oil
2 to 2½ pounds boneless lamb, cubed
2 tablespoons butter
1 medium-sized onion, diced
1½ cups uncooked rice
1½ teaspoons salt
¼ teaspoon basil
½ teaspoon oregano
1 can (8 ounces) tomato sauce
2 cups stock from lamb bones (or bouillon)
1 can onion soup (optional)
1 jar (4 ounces) pimiento

Heat oil in heavy skillet; brown lamb cubes. Remove meat and pour off all drippings. Melt butter and cook onion slowly until golden. Add rice, salt, basil, and oregano; cook until rice is lightly browned. Add lamb, tomato sauce, the liquids, and pimiento, and simmer 5 minutes. Pour in 3-quart casserole, cover and bake in oven at 350° for 1½ hours or until liquid is absorbed.

❉

Indian Lamb Curry

Makes 6 servings

2 tablespoons butter	2 teaspoons salt
1½ pounds lamb shoulder, cubed	2 cups stock or bouillon
1 cup chopped onion	2 tablespoons lemon juice
1 cup chopped apple	1 clove garlic, crushed
3 tablespoons all-purpose flour	⅓ cup seedless raisins
1 tablespoon curry powder	¼ cup chutney
	¼ cup chopped almonds
	Cooked rice

Cook lamb in butter over medium heat until browned on all sides. Add onion and apple and cook 5 minutes. Add flour, curry powder, and salt; mix well. Gradually add stock or bouillon and cook until thickened, stirring constantly. Add lemon juice, garlic, raisins, chutney, and almonds. Cover and cook over low heat 1 hour, stirring occasionally. Serve on rice. Serve with pimiento-stuffed olives, chutney, kumquats, sieved egg yolks, chopped green pepper, and toasted flaked coconut, as desired.

❉

Lamb with Persian Rhubarb Sauce (Khoreshe Rivas)

Makes 4 servings

2½ cups sliced fresh rhubarb°
¾ cup sugar
¾ cup and 1 tablespoon water
¼ cup butter
1 pound lamb, cut in 1-inch cubes
1 large onion, chopped
1 teaspoon salt
¼ to ½ teaspoon black pepper
½ teaspoon ground cinnamon
¼ teaspoon ground nutmeg
1 cup chopped parsley
1 tablespoon cornstarch
2 cups hot cooked rice

Place rhubarb in bowl; stir in sugar and ¾ cup water; set aside for 30 minutes; drain, reserving syrup. In 10-inch skillet, melt butter; sauté lamb, onion, and seasonings until meat is browned on all sides. Stir in parsley and sauté a few minutes more. Stir in rhubarb syrup. Simmer gently, covered, 40 minutes. Stir in drained rhubarb. Continue simmering, covered, 20 to 30 minutes or until meat is tender. Combine cornstarch and 1 tablespoon water. Stir into meat mixture; cook gently 2 to 3 minutes longer, until meat mixture is thickened. Serve over hot cooked rice.

° In place of fresh rhubarb, 1 can (1 pound) colored rhubarb may be used. In so doing, use ½ cup water and omit sugar.

❁

Planover Dishes

❧❧❧❧❧❧❧❧❧❧❧❧❧❧❧❧❧❧❧❧

When you roast a leg of lamb you will be doubly rewarded by the interesting, quick-to-fix dishes you can make from the leftover meat. Plan to have cooked meat left after the first meal. "Planovers" are time savers—and fun to serve.

Now, for a few specific recipes to try!

Lamb Asparagus Bake

Makes 4 servings

3 cups cooked rice
1 package (10 ounces) frozen asparagus
2 cups diced cooked lamb
1 can (10½ ounces) condensed cream of celery soup

1 cup water
1 teaspoon dehydrated minced onion
⅛ teaspoon pepper

Arrange rice in greased 2-quart casserole. Top with asparagus and lamb. Combine remaining ingredients; blend. Pour over lamb. Cover and bake in moderate (350°) oven 20 minutes. Uncover and bake 30 minutes.

❉

Hong Kong Lamb Chow Mein

Makes 6 servings

- 1 tablespoon butter
- 1 small green pepper, cut in strips
- ½ cup chopped scallions
- ½ cup diagonally sliced celery
- 1 package (10 ounces) frozen green peas
- 1 cup water
- 1 tablespoon cornstarch
- 2 cups diced cooked lamb
- ¼ teaspoon monosodium glutamate
- ¼ teaspoon salt
- ¼ teaspoon pepper
- 1 tablespoon soy sauce
- 1 can (1 pound) meatless chow mein
- Hot cooked rice
- Chinese noodles

Melt butter in skillet and sauté green pepper, scallions, celery, and green peas just until crisp-tender. Mix water with cornstarch and stir into skillet; cook slowly and stir 5 minutes longer or until thickened. Add lamb and seasonings; mix well and add chow mein vegetables. Heat and serve with rice and Chinese noodles.

❋

Calcutta Curry

Makes 4 to 6 servings

- ¼ cup salad oil
- 2 large onions, coarsely chopped
- 1½ cups coarsely chopped celery
- 1 cup seedless raisins
- 1 cup water
- 4 cups diced cooked lamb
- 1½ cups lamb stock or chicken bouillon
- 1½ cups chopped green apple
- ¼ cup curry powder (or to taste)
- Hot cooked rice

Heat oil; add onion and celery and cook until tender. Add raisins, water, diced lamb, and 1 cup lamb stock or bouillon to celery mixture. Cook, covered, 35 minutes over low heat. Add apple, curry powder, and remaining ½ cup stock or bouillon. Mix well and cook, covered, 10 minutes or until apple is tender. Serve over rice. Serve with accompaniments, such as chopped toasted almonds, chutney, sieved egg yolk, and kumquats, as desired.

❁

Lamb Divan

Makes 4 servings

2 tablespoons butter
2 tablespoons flour
1 cup milk
1¼ cup grated processed American cheese
½ teaspoon salt
¼ teaspoon celery seed
¼ teaspoon dry mustard

⅛ teaspoon pepper
½ teaspoon Worcestershire sauce
1 pound cooked sliced lamb
1 package (10 ounces) frozen broccoli, cooked
1 medium-sized tomato, sliced

Melt butter in saucepan; blend in flour. Gradually add milk, stirring constantly, and cook until thickened. Add 1 cup grated cheese, salt, celery seed, mustard, pepper, and Worcestershire sauce; stir until cheese is melted. Arrange layers of lamb, broccoli, and tomato slices in 1½ quart shallow baking dish. Pour sauce over all; bake in oven at 350° for 15 minutes. Sprinkle top with remaining ¼ cup grated cheese; bake 5 minutes longer.

❁

Lamb Tetrazzini

Makes 8 to 10 servings

1 pound spaghetti
½ pound mushrooms, thinly sliced
3 tablespoons butter
1 can (10½ ounces) condensed cream of celery soup
1 cup milk
1 cup heavy cream
3 tablespoons sherry

1 teaspoon salt
¼ teaspoon pepper
⅛ teaspoon nutmeg
2 pounds cooked lamb, cut into 2-inch strips, ½ inch thick (about 4 cups)
½ cup grated Parmesan cheese

Cook spaghetti according to package directions; drain. Meanwhile, cook mushrooms in butter over low heat until lightly browned; stir occasionally. Mix in soup, milk, cream, sherry, salt, pepper, and nutmeg; cook over low heat 10 minutes, stirring occasionally. Toss sauce with spaghetti and lamb. Turn into greased 3-quart baking dish. Sprinkle with Parmesan cheese; bake in oven at 350° for 25 minutes or until lightly browned.

❂

Lamb Bean Bake

Makes 4 servings

1 can (1 pound) baked beans
1 medium-sized onion, chopped

8 slices cooked lamb
¼ pound sliced Swiss cheese

Combine beans and onion; mix well. Arrange layers of bean mixture, lamb, and cheese in lightly greased 1½-quart baking dish. Bake in oven at 325° for 45 minutes.

❀

Mediterranean Lamb Pie

Makes 4 servings

2 cups water
2 vegetable-bouillon cubes
1 medium-sized zucchini, coarsely chopped
½ cup chopped scallion
½ teaspoon rosemary
1 teaspoon salt
¼ teaspoon pepper
⅓ cup dry sauterne or other dry white wine

⅓ cup flour
¼ cup catsup
3 cups diced cooked lamb
1 can (6 ounces) tomato paste
1 can (12 ounces) whole-kernel corn, drained
Pie pastry
Milk

Combine water and bouillon cubes in saucepan; bring to a boil. Add zucchini, scallion, rosemary, salt, and pepper; cook 5 minutes or until zucchini is tender. Blend sauterne, flour, and catsup together; stir into liquid in saucepan. Add lamb, tomato paste, and corn; cook until thickened. Turn into four 10-ounce custard cups, four 6-inch pie plates, or one 10-inch pie plate. Cover with pastry; brush with milk, and prick with fork. Bake in oven at 400° for 15 to 20 minutes or until crust is golden brown.

❀

Broiled Lamb-Stuffed Peppers

Makes 6 servings

3 medium-sized green
peppers
½ teaspoon salt
½ teaspoon celery seed
1 medium-sized onion,
chopped
2 tablespoons grated
Parmesan cheese

3 tablespoons French
dressing
2½ cups ground cooked
lamb
1 tablespoon chopped
parsley

Cut peppers in halves and remove seeds. Cook in small
amount of boiling salted water until tender. Drain. Combine
remaining ingredients; mix well. Fill peppers with lamb
mixture. Broil, 3 to 4 inches from source of heat, about
12 minutes or until done.

❀

Lamb Rice Luau

Makes 6 servings

¼ cup butter
¼ cup flour
½ teaspoon salt
¼ teaspoon pepper
2 vegetable bouillon
cubes
2½ cups water
1½ teaspoons soy sauce
¼ cup raisins

¼ cup toasted diced
almonds
2 cups cubed cooked lamb
½ large green pepper, cut
in strips
1 package (6 ounces)
curried rice
¼ cup chopped chutney

Melt butter in skillet and blend in flour, salt, and pepper.
Add bouillon cubes, water, and soy sauce and cook over
low heat, stirring constantly until thickened. Add raisins,
almonds, lamb, and green pepper. Stir well and simmer
10 to 15 minutes. Meanwhile, cook curried rice according
to package directions. Stir chutney into meat sauce. Place
rice in center of large heated platter and surround with
lamb sauce.

❃

Lamb-Stuffed Peppers

Makes 4 servings

4 large green peppers	1½ cups diced cooked lamb
2 tablespoons olive or salad oil	1 can (8 ounces) tomato sauce
¼ cup chopped onion	1 teaspoon garlic salt
¾ cup cooked diced carrots	½ teaspoon oregano
3 cups cooked rice	Salt and pepper to taste

Cut tops from green peppers. Remove seeds and membrane.
Cook green peppers, covered, in small amount of boiling
salted water for 10 minutes. Drain. Combine oil and onion
and sauté until lightly browned. Add carrots and rice
and cook over low heat, stirring frequently, until rice is
lightly browned. Add remaining ingredients; mix well.
Fill green peppers with lamb mixture. Place in lightly
greased shallow baking pan. Bake in oven at 350° for
45 minutes.

❃

Individual Lamb Pies

Makes 4 servings

3 tablespoons butter	2 cups diced cooked
3 tablespoons and 1 cup	lamb
sifted all-purpose flour	1½ cups sliced cooked
1½ cups lamb stock or	carrots
bouillon	1½ cups cooked peas
1½ teaspoons salt	⅓ cup shortening
¼ teaspoon pepper	¼ cup milk
¼ teaspoon rosemary	

Melt butter; add 3 tablespoons flour and blend. Gradually add stock or bouillon and cook over low heat, stirring constantly, until thickened. Add 1 teaspoon salt, pepper, rosemary, lamb, carrots, and peas; mix well. Turn into four individual baking dishes. Combine remaining 1 cup flour and ½ teaspoon salt. Cut in shortening. Add milk and mix lightly. Press into ball. Roll out on lightly floured surface to ⅛-inch thickness. Cut into four rounds. Place on lamb mixture. Seal edges. Bake in oven at 450° for 15 minutes or until lightly browned.

❧

Lamb Hash

Makes 4 servings

¼ cup butter	1 can (10½ ounces)
1 cup sliced onion	condensed cream of
3 cups diced cooked	celery soup
potatoes	1 teaspoon salt
2 cups diced cooked lamb	¼ teaspoon pepper

Melt butter; add onion and potatoes and cook 10 minutes over low heat, stirring occasionally. Add remaining ingredients; mix well. Cover and cook 15 minutes over low heat, stirring occasionally.

❄

Lamb Curry Bake

Makes 4 servings

2 cups diced cooked lamb	1 can (10½ ounces) condensed cream of mushroom soup
1 teaspoon onion juice	
½ cup sliced celery	1½ cups all-purpose flour
¼ teaspoon salt	½ teaspoon salt
¼ teaspoon pepper	2 teaspoons curry powder
⅓ cup milk	½ cup shortening
	3 tablespoons water

Combine lamb, onion juice, celery, salt, pepper, milk, and soup in lightly greased 10-inch pie plate. Sift flour, ½ teaspoon salt, and curry powder together. Cut in shortening. Add water; stir until well mixed. Roll out on lightly floured surface to ⅛-inch thickness. Place over lamb mixture. Seal and flute edge; slit top. Bake in oven at 400° for 35 minutes or until lightly browned.

❄

Spanish Rice with Lamb

Makes 4 servings

2 tablespoons butter
1 cup chopped onion
1 medium-sized green pepper, chopped
2 cups diced cooked lamb
3 medium-sized tomatoes, diced
½ cup water

1 beef-bouillon cube
1 teaspoon salt
¼ teaspoon powdered cloves
1 bay leaf
1 cup packaged precooked rice

Melt butter; add onion, green pepper, lamb, and tomatoes. Cook 15 minutes over low heat, stirring occasionally. Add water, bouillon cube, salt, cloves, and bay leaf. Cover and cook 25 minutes over low heat, stirring occasionally. If necessary, add small amount of additional water. Increase heat to boiling point, stirring constantly. Add rice; mix well. Remove from heat. Cover and let stand 5 minutes.

❊

Lamb Creole

Makes 4 servings

2 tablespoons butter
1 medium-sized onion, chopped
2 cups diced cooked lamb
1 can (1 pound) tomatoes
2 cups stock or bouillon

⅛ teaspoon cayenne
1 teaspoon salt
⅛ teaspoon crushed chili pepper
½ teaspoon garlic salt
1 cup rice

Melt butter; add onion and lamb and cook 5 minutes over low heat, stirring occasionally. Add undrained tomatoes, stock or bouillon, cayenne, salt, chili pepper, and garlic salt;

mix well. Cover and cook 20 minutes over low heat, stirring occasionally. Add rice. Cook over medium heat to boiling point. Stir. Cover and cook 20 minutes or until rice is done, stirring occasionally.

❖

Lamb Pie with Potato-Cheese Crust

Makes 4 servings

- ¼ cup butter
- 1 medium-sized onion, sliced
- ¼ pound mushrooms, sliced
- 2 tablespoons all-purpose flour
- 1 teaspoon salt

- ¼ teaspoon pepper
- ¼ teaspoon dry mustard
- 1 cup stock or bouillon
- 2 cups diced cooked lamb
- 3 cups seasoned mashed potatoes
- 2 cups (about ½ pound) grated Cheddar cheese

Melt butter; add onion and mushrooms and cook 5 minutes over low heat, stirring occasionally. Add flour, salt, pepper, and mustard; blend. Gradually add stock or bouillon and cook over low heat, stirring constantly, until thickened. Add lamb; mix well. Turn into 2-quart casserole. Combine potatoes and cheese; mix well. Top lamb mixture with potato mixture. Bake in oven at 350° for 30 minutes.

❖

Shepherd's Pie

Makes about 6 servings

2 packages quick-frozen whipped potatoes

¾ cup grated Cheddar cheese

1 package (10 ounces) frozen Brussels sprouts

2 cups diced cooked lamb

1 tablespoon all-purpose flour

2 tablespoons fat or oil

2 cups well-seasoned gravy

¾ cup drained cooked small onions

1 cup drained cooked sliced carrots

¼ cup canned pimiento strips

Salt and pepper to taste

Prepare potatoes following package directions. Add cheese to potatoes; mix. Prepare Brussels sprouts following package directions. Drain, if necessary. Coat lamb with flour. Heat fat or oil and add lamb. Cook over medium heat until lamb is browned. Add gravy, Brussels sprouts, onions, carrots, pimientos, and salt and pepper to taste; stir. Heat to serving temperature, stirring frequently. Turn into greased 2½ quart casserole. Top with a ring of potato mixture. Bake in oven at 425° for 15 minutes or until potatoes are lightly browned.

❀

Lamb Shanks

Lamb shanks are usually cut from the forequarter of the lamb, but they may also be taken from the shank end of leg of lamb. Both kinds may be used in any of the following recipes. Shanks vary somewhat in weight but will usually average about one pound. Because of the large bone a one-pound shank is not too large for most individual servings.

Tasty Lamb Shanks

Makes 4 servings

2 tablespoons salad oil
4 lamb shanks
1 clove garlic, finely chopped
½ pound mushrooms, sliced
1 can (6 ounces) tomato paste
⅓ cup molasses
1 cup bouillon
Salt and pepper to taste

Heat oil; add lamb shanks, garlic, and mushrooms. Cook until lamb shanks are browned on all sides. Combine remaining ingredients; blend. Pour over lamb mixture. Cover and cook over low heat for 1 hour or until lamb is tender.

Braised Lamb Shanks

Makes 4 servings

¼ cup all-purpose flour
1 teaspoon salt
¼ teaspoon pepper
¼ teaspoon thyme
⅛ teaspoon oregano
⅛ teaspoon basil
4 lamb shanks
2 tablespoons butter
1 large onion, sliced

1 small clove garlic, finely chopped
1 large green pepper, cut in strips
1½ cups stock or bouillon
¼ cup chopped canned pimientos
2 tablespoons water
Cooked rice

Combine flour, salt, pepper, thyme, oregano, and basil; mix well. Coat lamb on all sides with flour mixture; reserve remaining flour. Melt butter; add lamb and cook over low heat until browned on all sides. Add onion, garlic, and green pepper and cook 5 minutes. Add stock or bouillon and cook, covered, over low heat for 40 minutes. Add pimientos. Combine remaining flour mixture and water; mix well. Remove lamb and arrange on serving plate. Add flour mixture to stock or bouillon mixture. Cook over low heat, stirring constantly, until slightly thickened. Serve lamb shanks and sauce with rice.

❖

Broiled Lamb Shanks

Makes 4 servings

½ cup orange juice
⅛ teaspoon nutmeg
2 tablespoons grated orange rind

4 lamb shanks
1 medium-sized orange, sliced

Combine orange juice, nutmeg, and orange rind; mix well. Add lamb. Chill 1 hour, turning lamb occasionally. Remove lamb; reserve orange-juice mixture. Broil lamb, 4 to 5 inches from source of heat, 10 to 12 minutes. Turn. Brush with orange-juice mixture. Broil 10 to 12 minutes or until lamb is tender. Garnish with orange slices, if desired.

❁

Lamb Shanks with a Difference

Makes 6 servings

1 cup soy sauce	6 lamb shanks
¼ cup firmly packed brown sugar	2 tablespoons salad oil
⅓ cup sherry	2¼ cups water
¼ cup aniseed (tied in cheesecloth)	¼ cup cornstarch
	Hot cooked noodles or rice

Combine soy sauce, sugar, sherry, and aniseed; pour over lamb and marinate overnight. Drain lamb and brown on all sides in hot oil in large skillet; drain off drippings. Add marinade with aniseed bag; bring to boil and simmer 10 minutes. Add 2 cups of the water; cover and simmer 1 hour or until lamb is tender; remove lamb and keep warm. Mix cornstarch with remaining ¼ cup water; stir into skillet. Cook over low heat, stirring constantly until mixture thickens and boils one minute; remove aniseed bag. Serve lamb and sauce over noodles or rice.

❁

Holiday Lamb Shanks

Makes 4 servings

2 tablespoons salad oil
4 lamb shanks
1 medium-sized onion, sliced
1 medium-sized green pepper, chopped
¼ cup sifted unbleached flour

½ teaspoon basil
½ teaspoon thyme
1 teaspoon salt
¼ teaspoon pepper
½ cup stock or bouillon
1 cup burgundy

Heat oil. Add lamb, onion, and green pepper and cook over low heat until lamb is browned on all sides. Combine flour, basil, thyme, salt, and pepper; mix well. Gradually add stock or bouillon, stirring constantly until blended. Add flour mixture and burgundy to lamb; mix. Cover and cook over low heat, stirring occasionally, for 1½ hours or until lamb is tender.

❁

Lamb Shanks Español

Makes 6 servings

3 tablespoons olive oil
6 lamb shanks
2 cloves garlic
1 medium-sized onion, chopped
1 can (1 pound, 4 ounces) tomatoes

1 teaspoon salt
¼ teaspoon pepper
2 tablespoons water
2 tablespoons flour
¼ cup sliced pimiento-stuffed olives
3 cups hot cooked rice

Heat oil in large skillet; add lamb and garlic. Cook until lamb is browned on all sides; drain off drippings and remove garlic. Add onion, tomatoes, salt, and pepper to lamb. Cover and cook over low heat 1½ hours or until lamb is tender. Remove lamb from skillet. Blend water into flour; stir in some of hot liquid from skillet, then gradually return to skillet, stirring constantly. Add olives and lamb; simmer 5 minutes. Serve lamb shanks and sauce with rice.

❉

Lamb Shanks with Onion Sauce

Makes 4 servings

¼ cup all-purpose flour
1 teaspoon paprika
1 teaspoon salt
¼ teaspoon pepper
4 lamb shanks
2 tablespoons salad oil

3 medium-sized onions, sliced
1 cup stock or chicken bouillon
Cooked rice

Combine flour, paprika, salt, and pepper; mix well. Coat lamb on all sides with flour mixture; reserve flour mixture. Heat oil. Add lamb and cook over low heat until browned on all sides. Add onions and cook 5 minutes. Add stock or bouillon. Cover and cook over low heat 45 minutes or until lamb is tender. Remove lamb. Add remaining flour mixture to stock or bouillon mixture; blend. Cook over low heat, stirring constantly, until thickened. Serve lamb and onion sauce over rice.

❉

Lamb Shank Stew

Makes 4 servings

⅓ cup all-purpose flour
¼ teaspoon pepper
1 teaspoon salt
½ teaspoon chili powder
4 lamb shanks
2 tablespoons salad oil

1 medium-sized onion,
    sliced
¼ pound mushrooms,
    sliced
1 cup stock or bouillon
1 can (1 pound) tomatoes
Seasoned mashed potatoes

Combine flour, pepper, salt, and chili powder; mix well.
Coat lamb with flour mixture; reserve remaining flour
mixture. Heat oil. Add lamb and cook until browned on all
sides. Add onion and mushrooms and cook 5 minutes,
stirring occasionally. Add stock or bouillon and undrained
tomatoes. Cover and cook over low heat for 45 minutes
or until tender. Remove lamb. Gradually add remaining
flour mixture; mix well. Cook over low heat, stirring
constantly, until thickened. Serve lamb and mushroom sauce
with mashed potatoes.

❁

Baked Lamb-Shank Dinner

Makes 4 servings

2 tablespoons salad or
    olive oil
4 lamb shanks
2 cups stock or bouillon
3 bay leaves
1 teaspoon rosemary
½ teaspoon oregano
2 teaspoons salt

¼ teaspoon pepper
4 small potatoes, pared
4 medium-sized onions
4 medium-sized carrots
2 tablespoons all-purpose
    flour
½ cup water

Heat oil; add lamb and cook over low heat until browned on all sides. Add stock or bouillon, bay leaves, rosemary, oregano, salt, and pepper. Turn into roasting pan. Add vegetables. Cover and bake in oven at 325° for 2 hours or until vegetables are tender. Remove lamb and vegetables. Combine flour and water. Add to stock mixture and cook over medium heat, stirring constantly, until thickened. Serve gravy over lamb and vegetables.

❁

Grecian-Style Lamb Shanks

Makes 6 servings

6 lamb shanks	1 tablespoon lemon juice
2½ teaspoons salt	3 medium-sized onions,
2 teaspoons coriander	sliced
½ teaspoon pepper	1½ cups chopped scallions
2 tablespoons butter	3 egg yolks
2 cups water	6 lemon slices

Sprinkle lamb shanks with salt, coriander, and pepper. Brown well in butter in skillet. Add water and lemon juice; cover and simmer 1½ hours. Add onions and scallions; simmer ½ hour longer or until lamb is fork-tender. Remove meat, onions, and scallions to heated platter. Beat egg yolks with 1 tablespoon warm water and gradually add to skillet, stirring rapidly. Cook over low heat, stirring until thickened; add lemon slices and pour over lamb shanks.

❁

Lamb Shanks & Spinach

Makes 4 servings

¼ cup all-purpose flour
1 teaspoon salt
Dash pepper
4 lamb shanks
¼ cup shortening
1 medium-sized onion,
  sliced

1 can (10½ ounces)
  condensed cream of
  mushroom soup
½ cup water
1 teaspoon rosemary
1 package (10 ounces)
  frozen spinach
2 medium-sized tomatoes,
  cut in wedges

Combine flour, salt, and pepper. Coat lamb with flour
mixture. Melt shortening; add lamb and cook until browned
on all sides. Add onion, soup, water, and rosemary. Cover
and cook over low heat about 1 hour or until lamb is
tender. Add spinach and tomatoes. Cover and cook
about 15 minutes.

❁

Lamb Shanks & Fruit

Makes 4 servings

2 tablespoons butter
4 lamb shanks
1 medium-sized green
  pepper, cut in strips
1 medium-sized onion,
  chopped

2 cups orange juice
1 can (13½ ounces)
  frozen pineapple
  chunks, thawed
¼ cup cornstarch
Cooked rice

Melt butter; add lamb and cook over low heat until lamb
is browned on all sides. Add green pepper and onion and
cook 5 minutes. Add orange juice and mix well. Cover and
cook 40 minutes over low heat. Drain pineapple; reserve

syrup. Combine pineapple syrup and cornstarch; blend. Add pineapple-syrup mixture to lamb mixture. Cook over low heat, stirring constantly, until thickened. Add pineapple chunks and cook 5 minutes. Serve lamb and fruit over rice.

❄

Lamb Shanks in Cranberry Sauce

Makes 4 servings

2 tablespoons salad oil
4 lamb shanks

1 can (1 pound) jellied cranberry sauce

Heat oil. Add lamb and cook until browned on all sides. Drain off drippings, if necessary. Add cranberry sauce; stir until melted. Cover and cook over low heat 1 hour or until lamb is tender. Serve sauce with lamb.

❄

Corn-Lamb Stew

Makes 4 servings

2 tablespoons butter
4 lamb shanks
1 medium-sized green pepper, chopped
1 tablespoon dehydrated minced onion

1 can (1 pound) cream-style corn
Salt and pepper to taste
2 medium-sized tomatoes, cut in wedges

Melt butter; add lamb and cook over low heat, turning occasionally, until lightly browned on all sides. Add green pepper and onion and cook 5 minutes. Add corn, salt and pepper. Cover and cook over low heat 45 minutes or until lamb is tender. Add tomatoes and cover; cook 5 minutes.

❄

Pineapple Barbecued Lamb Shanks

Makes 4 servings

1 can (8¾ ounces)   ⅛ teaspoon pepper
   crushed pineapple   ¼ teaspoon cinnamon
¼ cup lemon juice   4 lamb shanks
1 teaspoon salt

Combine undrained pineapple, lemon juice, salt, pepper, and cinnamon; mix well. Brush lamb shanks with pineapple mixture. Broil, 3 to 4 inches from source of heat, or cook on outdoor grill 20 to 25 minutes or until lamb is tender. Turn lamb shanks and brush with pineapple mixture frequently during cooking period.

❖

Lamb-Neck Slices
in Main Dishes

❀❀❀❀❀❀❀ ❀❀❀❀❀❀❀ ❀❀❀❀❀

Lamb-neck slices are among the most economical cuts of lamb on the market. They are ideal for many braised or stewed dishes as well as for stock and casseroles.

In the following pages you will discover many ways of using them appealingly, which will also make it possible for you to save money on the family budget.

Necks can be purchased whole for stock, in single slices, or in double (butterfly) slices. In creating butterfly slices, your butcher will cut almost through the double slice and spread the meat open to form a butterfly shape.

Lamb-and-Vegetable Bake I

Makes 4 servings

- 1 large onion, sliced
- 1 large tomato, sliced
- ½ cup chopped celery
- 4 lamb-neck slices, about 1 inch thick
- 1 teaspoon salt
- ¼ teaspoon pepper
- ½ cup stock or bouillon

Arrange onion, tomato, and celery in bottom of shallow baking dish. Top with lamb. Sprinkle with salt and pepper. Pour stock or bouillon over lamb and vegetables. Bake in oven at 350° for 30 to 45 minutes or until lamb is tender.

❀

Lamb-and-Vegetable Bake II

Makes 4 servings

- 4 lamb-neck slices, about ¾ inch thick
- 1 can (1 pound) mixed vegetables
- 2 beef-bouillon cubes
- ¼ teaspoon garlic salt
- ¼ teaspoon celery salt
- ¼ teaspoon salt
- ¼ teaspoon pepper

Arrange lamb in shallow baking pan. Drain vegetables; reserve vegetable liquid. Heat vegetable liquid to boiling point. Dissolve bouillon cubes in vegetable liquid. Add garlic salt, celery salt, salt, and pepper to bouillon mixture; mix well. Pour bouillon mixture over lamb. Bake in oven at 325° about 40 minutes. Add mixed vegetables and bake about 15 minutes or until lamb is tender. Baste lamb and vegetables with bouillon mixture frequently during baking period.

❀

Braised Butterfly Slices with Peas

Makes 4 servings

- 2 tablespoons salad oil
- 2 butterfly lamb-neck slices, about ¾ inch thick
- 1½ cups water
- 1 teaspoon salt
- ¼ teaspoon pepper
- ⅓ cup all-purpose flour
- 2 tablespoons prepared mustard
- 1 can (1 pound) peas

Heat salad oil; add lamb and cook over medium heat until lamb is browned on both sides. Add water, salt, and pepper. Cover and cook 40 minutes over low heat. Remove lamb. Blend flour and mustard into liquid. Stir in undrained peas. Cook over low heat, stirring constantly, until slightly thickened. Top with lamb and heat through.

❈

Dilled Lamb Slices

Makes 6 servings

- 2 tablespoons butter
- 6 lamb-neck slices, about ¾ inch thick
- 2 tablespoons lemon juice
- ½ cup chopped dill
- ½ teaspoon commercial Bouquet Garni for Lamb
- 1 tablespoon prepared mustard

Salt and pepper to taste

Melt butter; add lamb. Cook until browned on both sides. Combine remaining ingredients; blend. Add to lamb. Cover and cook over low heat for 30 minutes or until lamb is tender.

❈

Lamb-and-Brussels-Sprouts Fall Dinner

Makes 6 servings

2 tablespoons butter
6 lamb-neck slices, about ¾ inch thick
6 whole white onions
1½ cups stock or bouillon
1 bay leaf
1 teaspoon paprika
¾ teaspoon oregano
¼ teaspoon thyme
Salt and pepper to taste
2 packages (10 ounces each) frozen Brussels sprouts
1 canned pimiento, sliced
1½ tablespoons all-purpose flour
Cooked rice

Melt butter; add lamb and cook over low heat until browned on both sides. Add onions, stock or bouillon, bay leaf, paprika, oregano, thyme, and salt and pepper. Cook, covered, over low heat for 20 minutes. Add Brussels sprouts and pimiento. Cover and cook over low heat for 5 minutes or until Brussels sprouts are tender. Remove lamb and vegetables. Add flour to stock; blend. Cook over low heat, stirring constantly, until thickened. Serve braised lamb and Brussels sprouts with rice.

❈

Lamb Skillet

Makes 6 servings

2 tablespoons butter
6 lamb-neck slices, about ¾ inch thick
1 cup sliced onion
1½ cups sliced mushrooms
1½ cups stock or bouillon
1½ teaspoons salt
¼ teaspoon pepper
1 teaspoon oregano
½ teaspoon thyme
¼ cup all-purpose flour

Melt butter; add lamb, onion, and mushrooms. Cook over low heat until lamb is browned on both sides. Add 1¼ cups stock or bouillon, salt, pepper, oregano, and thyme; mix. Cover and cook 30 minutes over low heat. Remove lamb. Blend flour with remaining ¼ cup stock or bouillon. Add to mushroom mixture. Cook over low heat, stirring constantly, until slightly thickened. Add lamb. Cook 10 minutes over low heat, stirring occasionally.

❊

Lamb-Neck Slices
with Mushrooms & Rice

Makes 4 servings

¼ cup butter	1½ cups water
4 lamb-neck slices, about ½ inch thick	1 beef-bouillon cube
	½ cup rice
½ pound fresh mushrooms, sliced	¾ teaspoon salt
	⅛ teaspoon pepper
1 medium-sized onion, sliced	

Melt butter. Add lamb and cook over low heat until browned on both sides. Add mushrooms and onion and cook 5 minutes. Add water and bouillon cube. Cover and cook 10 minutes. Add rice, salt, and pepper; mix well. Cover and cook 20 minutes or until lamb and rice are tender.

❊

Lamb-Neck Slices
with Barbecue Sauce

Makes 4 servings

2 tablespoons salad oil
4 lamb-neck slices, about ¾ inch thick
6 tablespoons all-purpose flour
½ teaspoon onion salt
1 teaspoon salt
¼ teaspoon pepper
¼ cup water

2 tablespoons seedless raisins
¼ cup firmly packed brown sugar
1 can (8 ounces) tomato sauce
¼ cup vinegar
½ teaspoon ginger
2 cloves garlic, crushed

Heat oil. Add lamb and cook until browned on both sides; drain off drippings. Arrange lamb in shallow baking dish. Combine flour, onion salt, salt, and pepper; blend. Stir in water, raisins, brown sugar, tomato sauce, vinegar, ginger, and garlic. Pour over lamb. Bake in moderate (350°) oven 30 minutes or until tender.

❖

Spanish Lamb Slices

Makes 6 large servings

12 lamb-neck slices, 1 inch thick
3 tablespoons salad oil
1 medium-sized green pepper, chopped
3 cloves garlic, minced
1 can (1 pound, 4 ounces) tomatoes

1½ teaspoons salt
½ teaspoon marjoram
⅛ teaspoon pepper
1 teaspoon Worcestershire sauce
½ cup boiling water
2 cups precooked package rice

Brown lamb on both sides in hot oil; drain thoroughly. Add green pepper, garlic, tomatoes, salt, marjoram, pepper, and Worcestershire sauce; mix well. Cover and simmer over low heat for 30 to 45 minutes or until lamb is tender. Stir in water and rice; cover and let stand 5 minutes.

❁

Lamb Parmigiana

Makes 4 servings

½ cup fine dry bread crumbs	4 lamb-neck slices, about ¾ inch thick
¼ cup and 2 teaspoons grated Parmesan cheese	3 tablespoons cooking oil
¼ teaspoon rosemary	1 can (10½ ounces) meatless spaghetti sauce
1 egg	¼ pound mozzarella cheese

Combine bread crumbs, ¼ cup grated Parmesan cheese, and rosemary. Mix well. Beat egg slightly. Dip lamb-neck slices in egg and coat with bread-crumb mixture. Heat the cooking oil; add lamb and cook until browned on both sides. Arrange lamb in shallow baking pan. Pour half of the can of spaghetti sauce around lamb. Slice mozzarella cheese and place cheese slices over lamb. Pour remaining spaghetti sauce over lamb. Sprinkle remaining two teaspoons grated Parmesan cheese over lamb. Bake in oven at 325° for 30 to 40 minutes or until lamb is tender.

❁

Lamb Broiler Meal

Makes 4 servings

4 lamb-neck slices, about 1 inch thick

2 medium-sized tomatoes, halved

3 cups seasoned mashed potatoes

Salt and pepper to taste

4 slices processed American cheese

Arrange lamb and tomato halves on aluminum foil-lined broiler pan. Pipe potatoes around tomato halves. Sprinkle lamb and tomato halves with salt and pepper. Broil, 3 to 4 inches from source of heat, 5 to 6 minutes. Turn lamb and broil 2 to 3 minutes. Top lamb with cheese and broil 3 to 4 minutes or until cheese melts.

❊

Paprika Lamb-Neck Slices

Makes 4 servings

2 tablespoons butter

4 lamb-neck slices, about ½ inch thick

1 medium-sized onion, chopped

1 cup chopped celery

½ teaspoon salt

¼ teaspoon pepper

2 teaspoons paprika

½ cup water

½ cup commercial sour cream

Melt butter. Add lamb and cook over low heat until browned on both sides. Add onion and celery and cook 5 minutes. Add salt, pepper, paprika, and water; mix well. Cover and cook over low heat 30 minutes. Gradually stir in sour cream. Heat through.

❊

Caraway-Flavored Lamb in Sour Cream

Makes 6 servings

6 lamb-neck slices, about ¾ inch thick
Seasoned flour
3 tablespoons salad oil
2 medium-sized onions, sliced
1 clove garlic, crushed
⅓ cup water
⅓ cup white vinegar
½ teaspoon caraway seeds

½ teaspoon oregano
2 tablespoons salt
4 to 6 quarts boiling water
1 pound (about 8 cups) wide egg noodles
1½ cups commercial sour cream
Paprika

Dredge lamb in seasoned flour. Heat salad oil; add lamb and cook over medium heat until browned on both sides. Drain off drippings. Add onions, garlic, water, vinegar, caraway seeds, and oregano. Cover and cook over low heat for 45 minutes or until lamb is tender.

Meanwhile, add 2 tablespoons salt to rapidly boiling water. Gradually add noodles so that water continues to boil. Cook uncovered, stirring occasionally, until tender. Drain in colander.

Add sour cream to lamb. Cover and cook 2 minutes. Serve lamb in sour cream over noodles and sprinkle with paprika.

❁

Lamb Tongues and Kidneys

❧❧❧❧❧❧❧❧❧❧❧❧❧❧❧❧❧❧

While not always easy to obtain, lamb tongues can be great delicacies. Be sure they are fresh when you buy them—then try them in these and other favorite tongue recipes.

Lamb-Tongue Aspic

Makes 8 to 10 servings

4 small lamb tongues	2 bay leaves
2 teaspoons peppercorns	Water to cover
1 tablespoon salt	

Simmer above ingredients until tongues are fork-tender. Pour off broth and allow tongues to cool. Peel off outer skin; slice in very thin slices. Chill in your favorite aspic.

✻

Lamb Tongues Vinaigrette

Excellent buffet item

1 or 2 tongues per person
Canned bouillon to cover,
   diluted with water
   according to directions
Herb bouquet (parsley,

celery leaves, a whole
   onion studded with
   cloves and one bay leaf)
Vinaigrette sauce (see
   below)

Cover tongues with bouillon, add seasonings, and simmer until tongues are tender (1 to 1½ hours). Drain and peel tongues, split lengthwise, and arrange in a shallow serving dish. Pour Vinaigrette Sauce over the tongues and refrigerate for 24 hours. Turn several times to keep meat coated with sauce.

Vinaigrette Sauce

For 2 pounds of tongue

½ cup olive oil (part can
   be salad oil)
3 tablespoons wine
   vinegar
1 teaspoon salt
Dash freshly ground pepper

1 teaspoon minced chives
1 teaspoon minced parsley
½ teaspoon minced
   tarragon
½ hard-cooked egg,
   chopped

Mix above ingredients.

❊

Tasty Baked Lamb Tongues

Makes 7 servings

2 packages lamb tongues,
    about 14 tongues
Water to cover
1 onion, sliced
4 cloves garlic
Salt to taste
1 teaspoon basil
1 teaspoon thyme
¼ teaspoon sage

Generous sprigs of parsley
1 package (12 or 14
    ounces) butterfly
    macaroni
½ cup sauterne
1 can (10 ounces)
    mushroom soup
Parmesan cheese

Cover lamb tongues with water and add onion, garlic, salt, basil, thyme, sage, and parsley. Simmer until tongues are ready to peel. Drain and reserve liquid. Peel tongues and slice. Cook and drain macaroni. In buttered baking dish, place tongue slices and macaroni in alternate layers. Pour liquid used in cooking lamb over layers; add wine and mushroom soup. The combination of liquid, wine, and soup should cover lamb and macaroni. Bake in oven at 400° until slightly browned on top. Sprinkle with Parmesan cheese and serve.

❖

Lamb Kidneys in Rice Ring

Makes 6 servings

1 cup butter
½ pound mushrooms, sliced
1 clove garlic, crushed
1 large onion, sliced
¼ teaspoon salt
⅛ teaspoon pepper

12 lamb kidneys, split and trimmed
1 tablespoon crushed rosemary
3 tablespoons lemon juice
Parsley Rice Ring (see below)

Melt butter in large skillet. Add mushrooms and cook quickly until tender; remove from skillet and keep warm. To hot butter in skillet, add garlic, onion, salt, and pepper; cook slowly until onion is lightly browned; remove onion from skillet and keep warm. Add kidneys to hot skillet and sprinkle with rosemary. Cook quickly, turning frequently, 7 to 9 minutes or until kidneys are tender but still pink in the center. Return mushrooms and onion to skillet; sprinkle with lemon juice and cook 5 minutes longer. Arrange kidneys, mushrooms, and onion in center of Parsley Rice Ring. Serve with butter sauce from skillet.

Parsley Rice Ring

Cook 2 cups rice according to package directions, using 4 cups chicken broth for liquid. Stir in ¼ cup butter or margarine and ½ cup finely chopped parsley. Pack with spoon into lightly oiled 5½-cup ring mold. Let stand 10 minutes; unmold onto serving plate.

❖

Ground Lamb

FRESH AND COOKED

Fresh or leftover ground lamb can provide the basis for many dishes. The recipes in this section apply to both fresh and cooked ground lamb. If fresh ground lamb is not available in your market when you want it, buy a shoulder and have it boned and ground, or cut the meat from the bones at home and put it in a meat grinder. Use the bones removed from the shoulder for the preparation of stock.

Some of the recipes in this section using fresh ground lamb can also be used with ground or finely diced cooked lamb from leftover roast. Fresh ground lamb usually requires no fat for frying. If it seems exceptionally lean, you may wish to use a tablespoonful or two. If the ground lamb you use contains considerable fat, drain after cooking to avoid excessive richness. Personal taste and judgment should serve as a guide in this matter.

Greek Lamb Dinner Tarts

Makes 8 tarts

¼ cup butter
½ cup chopped onion
2 pounds ground fresh lamb or the equivalent in finely diced cooked lamb
2 cans (6 ounces each) tomato paste
Salt and pepper to taste
8 eggs, beaten
2 cups fine dry bread crumbs
¼ cup chopped parsley
¼ teaspoon cinnamon
2 cups sifted all-purpose flour
1 teaspoon salt
⅔ cup shortening
1 cup grated Cheddar cheese, about ¼ pound
¼ cup water

Melt butter; add onion and cook until lightly browned. Add lamb and brown slightly. Drain off drippings. Add tomato paste, salt and pepper, eggs, bread crumbs, parsley, and cinnamon to lamb mixture; mix well. Pour into tart shells made as follows:

Sift flour and 1 teaspoon salt together. Cut in shortening. Add cheese and mix well. Gradually add water; mix well. Press into ball. Roll out on lightly floured surface to ⅛-inch thickness. Cut into eight 6½-inch rounds. Cut remaining pastry into desired shapes. Press rounds into 4½-inch tart pans. Fill with lamb mixture. Place pastry cut-outs on top. Bake in oven at 350° for 20 minutes.

❁

Pickle Lamb Cakes

Makes 12 cakes, about 6 servings

2 pounds ground lamb
1½ cups (3 slices bread) soft bread crumbs
1 egg
½ cup undrained sweet pickle relish
⅓ cup chopped onion
¾ cup milk

1½ teaspoons salt
½ teaspoon oregano
½ teaspoon garlic salt
¼ teaspoon pepper
3 to 4 cups mashed potatoes*
12 small sweet gherkins
Carrot slivers

Mix together lamb, bread crumbs, egg, relish, onion, milk, and seasonings. Press into twelve 3-inch muffin pans. Bake 40 minutes in moderate (350°) oven. Drain off drippings. Place meat loaves on plank. Pipe mashed potatoes around edge of plank and on top of each meat cake. Broil about 2 minutes or until potatoes are lightly browned.

Make pickle candles by cutting a slit in one end of each sweet gherkin and inserting carrot slivers. Place "candles" on potato rosettes atop the meat cakes.

* Use about 3 pounds potatoes or 1 package (6 ounces) instant mashed potatoes, prepared according to package directions.

❄

Lamb Patties with Tomato Sauce

Makes 6 servings

1 pound ground fresh
lamb or coarsely ground
cooked lamb
½ cup fine dry bread
crumbs
1 egg, beaten
1 teaspoon salt

¼ teaspoon pepper
1 teaspoon dehydrated
minced onion
½ teaspoon thyme
1 can (8 ounces) tomato
sauce

Combine lamb, bread crumbs, egg, salt, pepper, onion, and
thyme; mix well. Shape into six patties. Cook over low
heat about 5 to 6 minutes on each side. Drain patties on
absorbent paper. Meanwhile, heat tomato sauce. Serve
patties with sauce.

❁

Lamb-Pineapple Patties

Makes 8 servings

2 pounds ground lamb°
1 can (9 ounces) pineapple

slices, drained and cut in
half
2 tablespoons apricot jam

Shape lamb into eight patties. Cook about 10 minutes over
low heat until browned on both sides. Top with pineapple
slices and jam. Cover and cook 5 minutes.

° If frozen lamb patties are used, cover and cook 20 minutes or until
browned on both sides. Add pineapple slices and jam. Cover and cook
5 minutes.

❁

Crunchy Lamb & Pineapple Patties

Makes 4 servings

1 can (5 ounces) water
   chestnuts
1 pound ground lamb
1 egg, beaten
1 tablespoon chopped
   chives
½ teaspoon salt
½ teaspoon onion salt
⅛ teaspoon ginger

½ teaspoon soy sauce
1 can (9 ounces)
   pineapple slices
1 teaspoon cornstarch
2 teaspoons lemon juice
Dash pepper
Parsley
Radish roses

Drain and chop water chestnuts; reserve liquid. Combine
lamb, egg, chives, salt, onion salt, ginger, soy sauce, and
2 tablespoons chestnut liquid; mix lightly and shape into
four rectangles (4½ x 3 inches). Broil lamb, 3 to 4 inches
from source of heat, 5 to 7 minutes on each side.

Meanwhile, drain pineapple; blend syrup with cornstarch
in saucepan. Add lemon juice, pepper, and remaining
chestnut liquid. Cook over low heat, stirring constantly,
until thickened. Cut pineapple slices in half and arrange
2 halves over each patty; broil 1 minute or until pineapple
is lightly browned. Pour pineapple sauce over patties;
garnish with parsley and radish roses.

❂

Lamb Meat Balls in Cream Sauce

Makes 4 servings

1 pound ground lamb
1 small onion, chopped
⅓ cup chopped green pepper
1 can (10½ ounces) condensed cream of mushroom soup

¼ cup milk
½ teaspoon salt
⅛ teaspoon pepper
Cooked rice

Shape lamb into 1½-inch balls. Cook over low heat until browned on all sides. Add onion and green pepper and cook 5 minutes. Add soup, milk, salt, and pepper; mix well. Cover and cook over low heat 30 minutes, stirring occasionally. Serve lamb and sauce over rice.

❁

Barbecued Lamb Meat Balls

Makes 4 servings

1 pound ground lamb
1 egg
¾ teaspoon garlic salt
⅓ cup fine dry bread crumbs
1 tablespoon butter

1 medium-sized onion, chopped
⅓ cup chopped green pepper
1 can (8 ounces) tomato sauce
¼ teaspoon dry mustard

Combine lamb, egg, ½ teaspoon garlic salt, and bread crumbs; mix well. Shape into eight balls. Broil, 3 to 4 inches from source of heat, or cook on outdoor grill 5 to 7 minutes; turn. Cook 5 to 7 minutes longer or until desired degree of doneness.

Meanwhile, melt butter; add onion and green pepper and cook 5 minutes over medium heat, stirring occasionally. Add tomato sauce, remaining ¼ teaspoon garlic salt, and mustard; mix well. Cook 10 minutes over low heat, stirring occasionally. Serve tomato mixture with lamb meat balls.

❁

Lamb Loaf with Chili Hollandaise

Makes 6 servings

1½ pounds ground lamb	1¼ teaspoons salt
⅓ cup milk	¼ teaspoon pepper
½ cup fine cracker crumbs	¼ cup chili sauce
1 medium-sized onion, chopped	1 jar (6 ounces) hollandaise sauce

Combine lamb, milk, crumbs, onion, salt, and pepper; mix well. Press into 9 x 5 x 3-inch loaf pan. Bake in oven at 350° for 1 hour or until done. Turn out of pan and drain off drippings.

Meanwhile, combine chili sauce and hollandaise sauce; mix well and simmer to heat through. Serve lamb loaf with sauce.

❁

Party-Perfect Lamb Loaf

Makes 6 servings

2 tablespoons chopped
  onion
2 tablespoons butter
2 cans (3 ounces each)
  chopped mushrooms
1/3 cup finely chopped
  cooked ham (optional)

1/4 cup fine dry bread
  crumbs
1/2 teaspoon salt
1/4 teaspoon pepper
2 tablespoons dry sherry
2 pounds lean ground
  lamb

Sauté onion in butter until tender. Add liquid from mushrooms. Finely chop mushrooms and add to onion mixture. Simmer until liquid is reduced to about 1 tablespoon. Remove from heat; add lamb, bread crumbs, salt, pepper, and sherry. Divide lamb into three parts. Layer lamb and mushroom mixture in 9 x 5 x 3-inch loaf pan, beginning and ending with lamb. Bake in oven at 350° for 1 hour, 15 minutes. Drain off drippings before serving.

❁

Cornbread-Topped Lamb Pie

Makes 6 servings

2 tablespoons chopped
  onion
1 tablespoon butter
1 1/2 pounds ground lamb
1 can (10 1/2 ounces)
  mushroom gravy
1 teaspoon salt
1/4 teaspoon pepper

1 tablespoon parsley flakes
1 teaspoon chervil
1/2 teaspoon crushed bay
  leaf
1 package (10 ounces)
  frozen mixed vegetables,
  cooked and drained
1 package (7 ounces)
  corn-muffin mix

In large skillet sauté onion in butter until crisp-tender.
Add lamb and sauté until lightly browned. Drain off excess
fat. Stir in mushroom gravy, salt, pepper, parsley, chervil,
and bay leaf. Simmer, uncovered, for 20 minutes. Add cooked
vegetables. Pour into 8-inch-square baking dish. Prepare
muffin mix according to package directions. Spread over
lamb mixture. Bake in a hot (400°) oven 35 minutes
or until done.

❂

Pignolia Lamb with Cottage Sauce

Makes 6 servings

1½ pounds ground lamb	3 tablespoons butter
½ cup chopped parsley	3 tablespoons flour
1 teaspoon seasoned salt	½ teaspoon salt
1 teaspoon turmeric	¼ teaspoon celery salt
2 tablespoons prepared horseradish	Dash pepper
	1½ cups milk
½ cup commercial sour cream	1 cup (8 ounces) cottage cheese
2 tablespoons pignolia nuts	8 ounces medium noodles, cooked
2 tablespoons salad oil	

Combine lamb, parsley, seasoned salt, ½ teaspoon turmeric,
horseradish, sour cream, and pignolia nuts; mix lightly with
fork and shape into 18 balls. Heat oil in skillet; brown lamb
well on all sides.

Meanwhile, melt butter in saucepan; blend in flour, salt,
½ teaspoon turmeric, celery salt, and pepper. Gradually
add milk and cook, stirring constantly, until thickened. Stir
in cottage cheese and heat to serving temperature. To serve,
arrange lamb on hot noodles; top with cottage cheese.

❂

Celia's Lamb-Stuffed Cabbage

Makes 6 servings

1 large head cabbage
1½ pounds lean ground lamb
½ cup fine dry bread crumbs
2 tablespoons finely minced onion
1 egg
Salt and pepper

2 cans (8 ounces each) tomato sauce
1 can (6 ounces) tomato paste
1 cup water
2 tablespoons lemon juice
2 tablespoons sugar
Raisin Rice (see below)

In large kettle, cook cabbage three minutes in boiling water. Combine lamb, bread crumbs, onion, egg, 1 teaspoon salt, and ¼ teaspoon pepper. Separate leaves (about 18); place a small amount of meat mixture in each leaf. Roll and secure with wooden pick. Combine tomato sauce and paste, water, lemon juice, sugar, and salt and pepper to taste in large kettle with stuffed cabbage. Simmer, covered, for 1½ hours. Serve over Raisin Rice.

Raisin Rice

Cook 1 cup raw rice according to package directions, adding ½ cup seedless raisins and ⅛ teaspoon grated lemon peel to raw rice.

❖

Lamb-Stuffed Cabbage

Makes 8 servings

1 small head cabbage
Boiling water to cover
1 pound ground lamb
8 tablespoons soft butter
2 eggs, 1 well beaten
2 small onions, finely
  chopped

1 cup raw rice
1 teaspoon salt
1 teaspoon ground
  cinnamon
1/4 cup pine nuts
2 tablespoons lemon juice
1/4 cup water

Place whole cabbage in large saucepan. Cover with boiling water and let stand about 5 minutes, until soft enough to separate the leaves. Drain and let cool enough to handle. Cut out hard stem end and carefully remove leaves, being sure to keep them as whole as possible.

Combine meat, 4 tablespoons of soft butter, the beaten egg, onions, rice, salt, cinnamon, and pine nuts. Blend thoroughly. Place a tablespoonful of the mixture in the center of each cabbage leaf; roll leaf around meat and tuck in the ends. Place rolls close together in a large saucepan. Dot with the remaining 4 tablespoons soft butter. Cover tightly; cook over low heat 30 minutes. Turn rolls, cover, and cook 30 minutes longer. Remove rolls to a warm serving platter.

Combine the egg, lemon juice, and water; beat slightly with beater. Slowly add to liquid in saucepan, stirring constantly. Pour over rolls and serve at once.

❇

Lamb Cheese Pie

Makes 4 servings

- 1 pound ground lamb or the equivalent in chopped cooked lamb
- 1 tablespoon dehydrated minced onion
- 4 eggs, slightly beaten
- 1½ cups grated Cheddar cheese
- ½ cup milk
- 1 teaspoon salt
- ¼ teaspoon pepper
- 1 unbaked 8-inch pastry shell
- 2 tablespoons chopped parsley

Cook lamb over low heat until browned, stirring occasionally. Drain off drippings. Combine lamb, onion, eggs, 1 cup cheese, milk, salt, and pepper; mix well. Turn into pastry shell. Top with remaining ½ cup cheese and parsley. Bake in oven at 400° for 40 minutes or until set.

❈

Little Pancakes with Curried Lamb

Makes 4 servings

- 2 tablespoons salad oil
- 1 pound ground lamb or the equivalent in finely chopped cooked lamb
- ⅓ cup all-purpose flour
- 1 tablespoon curry powder (or to taste)
- 2 cups stock or chicken bouillon
- 1 cup milk
- 1 egg, beaten
- 1 cup pancake mix
- 1 tablespoon melted butter
- ⅓ cup flaked coconut

Heat oil; add lamb and cook until browned, stirring occasionally. Drain off drippings if necessary. Combine flour and curry powder in small pan; slowly stir in stock or bouillon to blend. Cook over low heat, stirring constantly, until thickened. Add to lamb; cook 15 minutes over low heat, stirring occasionally.

Meanwhile, make pancakes. Combine milk, egg, pancake mix, butter, and coconut. Stir lightly until fairly smooth. Drop pancake batter, 2 tablespoons at a time, onto hot greased griddle. Bake until golden brown on both sides. Serve with lamb curry sauce.

❊

Spaghetti & Lamb Meat Balls

Makes 4 servings

1 pound ground lamb	½ teaspoon oregano
¼ cup coarsely chopped onion	3½ teaspoons salt
	Pepper to taste
½ cup chopped green pepper	½ teaspoon rosemary
	1 teaspoon sugar
2 cans (8 ounces each) tomato sauce	3 quarts boiling water
	8 ounces spaghetti

Shape lamb into balls. Cook over low heat until browned on all sides. Add onion and green pepper; cook 5 minutes. Combine tomato sauce, oregano, ½ teaspoon salt, pepper, rosemary, and sugar; pour over lamb. Cook, covered, over low heat for 1 hour.

Meanwhile, add 1 tablespoon salt to rapidly boiling water. Gradually add spaghetti so that water continues to boil. Cook uncovered, stirring occasionally, until tender. Drain in colander. Serve with lamb meat balls and sauce.

❊

Old-Fashioned Lamb-and-Cranberry Skillet

Makes 4 to 6 servings

1½ pounds ground lamb
1 egg
1 teaspoon salt
⅛ teaspoon pepper
¼ teaspoon rosemary
1½ cups fresh cranberries
¾ cup sugar
2 tablespoons lemon juice
3 cups cooked rice
2 tablespoons melted butter
1 tablespoon grated onion
1 teaspoon grated lemon rind
Salt and pepper to taste

Combine lamb, egg, 1 teaspoon salt, ⅛ teaspoon pepper, and rosemary; mix well. Shape into 1½-inch balls. Cook over low heat until browned on all sides. Drain off drippings.

Meanwhile, combine cranberries, sugar, and lemon juice. Cook over low heat until sugar is dissolved, stirring occasionally. Combine remaining ingredients; mix well. Add rice mixture and cranberry mixture to lamb balls. Cover and cook 30 minutes over low heat.

❖

Lamb-and-Vegetable Casserole

Makes 4 servings

1 pound ground lamb or the equivalent in finely diced cooked lamb
1 package (10 ounces) frozen mixed vegetables, thawed
Salt and pepper to taste
1 can (10½ ounces) condensed tomato soup
2 cups seasoned mashed potatoes

Brown lamb over low heat (using small amount of fat, if cooked lamb is used), stirring occasionally. Drain off drippings. Combine lamb, mixed vegetables, salt and pepper, and condensed soup; mix well. Arrange lamb mixture in greased 1½-quart casserole. Top with potatoes. Bake in oven at 350° for 30 minutes.

❀

Spaghetti with Lamb Sauce

Makes 6 servings

3½ teaspoons salt	3 tablespoons chopped parsley
3 quarts boiling water	1 pound ground lamb
8 ounces spaghetti	¼ teaspoon pepper
1 tablespoon salad oil	1 can (10½ ounces) condensed cream of mushroom soup
2 tablespoons chopped onion	

Add 3 teaspoons salt to rapidly boiling water. Gradually add spaghetti so that water continues to boil. Cook uncovered, stirring occasionally, until tender. Drain in colander.

Meanwhile, heat oil; add onion, 1 tablespoon parsley, lamb and ½ teaspoon salt and ¼ teaspoon pepper. Cook over medium heat until meat is browned. Add condensed soup; blend. Cover and cook 30 minutes over low heat, stirring occasionally. Serve spaghetti with lamb sauce. Garnish with remaining parsley.

❀

Lamb-Stuffed Zucchini

Makes 4 servings

4 medium-sized zucchini
1 pound ground lamb
2 tablespoons rice
Salt to taste

¼ teaspoon pepper
⅛ teaspoon allspice
1 can (1 pound, 3 ounces) tomatoes

Cut zucchini in half lengthwise; remove seeds leaving ¼-inch shell. Combine lamb, rice, salt, pepper, and allspice; mix well. Fill zucchini shells with lamb mixture. Place in skillet. Top with undrained tomatoes. Cover tightly and cook 45 minutes over medium heat. Serve stuffed zucchini with tomatoes.

❁

Italian-Dinner Lamburgers

Makes 4 servings

1 pound ground lamb
¾ teaspoon oregano
½ teaspoon salt
¼ teaspoon pepper
4 slices mozzarella cheese

1 can (8 ounces) tomato sauce
1 medium-sized green pepper, cut in strips
¼ cup chopped onion

Combine lamb, oregano, salt, and pepper; mix well. Shape into four patties. Broil, 3 to 4 inches from source of heat, 5 to 7 minutes. Turn. Broil 5 minutes. Top with cheese and broil 2 minutes or until cheese melts. Meanwhile, combine remaining ingredients; mix well. Cook 10 minutes over medium heat. Serve tomato sauce with patties.

❁

Plain Lamb Meat Loaf

Makes 4 servings

1 pound ground lamb
1 medium-sized onion, chopped
1 egg, beaten

2 cups soft bread crumbs
1 teaspoon salt
¼ teaspoon pepper
½ cup milk

Combine all ingredients; mix well. Press into 9 x 5 x 3-inch loaf pan. Bake in oven at 350° for 1 hour. Drain off drippings. Arrange on serving plate.

❁

Chili Lamb

Makes 4 to 6 servings

1 pound ground lamb
1 cup chopped onion
1 cup chopped celery
1 can (1 pound) red kidney beans
1 can (8 ounces) tomato sauce

1 tablespoon chili powder
1½ teaspoons salt
½ teaspoon oregano
¼ teaspoon basil
2 teaspoons sugar

Cook lamb, onion, and celery over low heat until lamb is browned, stirring occasionally. Add undrained beans and remaining ingredients. Cover and cook 45 minutes over low heat, stirring occasionally. Mixture will be thick. May be served with rice.

❁

Lamb Loaf with Glazed Apples

Makes 6 servings

1½ pounds ground lamb
¼ cup fine dry bread crumbs
1 egg, beaten
1¼ teaspoons salt
¼ teaspoon pepper

2 tablespoons chopped chives
¼ cup currant jelly, melted
2 tablespoons lemon juice
1 medium-sized apple, cored and cut in wedges

Combine lamb, bread crumbs, egg, salt, pepper, and chives; mix well. Shape into loaf. Place on rack in roasting pan. Bake in oven at 350° for 45 minutes. Combine remaining ingredients; mix well. Pour apple mixture over loaf and bake 15 minutes or until apples are tender.

❀

Lamb Quiche Lorraine

Makes 6 servings

¼ pound bacon, cooked
1 unbaked 9-inch pastry shell
1 pound ground lamb or the equivalent in finely diced cooked lamb
1 tablespoon butter

1 tablespoon all-purpose flour
⅔ cup hot milk
2 eggs, beaten
1 teaspoon salt
¼ teaspoon pepper

Arrange bacon on bottom of pastry shell. Cook lamb over medium heat until browned. Drain off drippings. Arrange lamb over bacon. Melt butter; add flour and blend. Add remaining ingredients; mix well. Pour over lamb. Bake in oven at 350° for 45 to 50 minutes or until set.

❀

Lamb & Noodles Romanoff

Makes 6 servings

1½ pounds ground lamb
½ teaspoon salt
¼ teaspoon pepper
½ teaspoon prepared
   mustard
¼ teaspoon
   Worcestershire sauce
1 medium-sized onion,
   chopped
1 clove garlic, crushed
1 egg

1 tablespoon butter
2 tablespoons chopped
   green pepper
1 teaspoon caraway seed
1 cup commercial sour
   cream
2 packages (5¾ ounces
   each) Noodles
   Romanoff mix
⅔ cup milk

In mixing bowl, combine lamb, salt, pepper, mustard, Worcestershire sauce, onion, garlic, and egg. Mix lightly and shape into small balls. Brown in butter in skillet. Add green pepper and caraway seed and cook 10 minutes longer. Drain off drippings; add sour cream and set aside.

Meanwhile, prepare noodles according to package directions. Drain and add to skillet with sauce mix (found in small envelope) and milk. Mix lightly and heat through, stirring as needed.

Lamb-and-Eggplant Bake

Makes 6 servings

⅓ cup butter
1 medium-sized eggplant, sliced lengthwise in ½-inch slices
1 pound ground lamb
¼ cup chopped onion
½ teaspoon salt

Dash pepper
1 can (8 ounces) tomato sauce
¼ cup grated Parmesan cheese
½ pound mozzarella cheese, sliced

Melt butter; add eggplant slices and cook over low heat until lightly browned on both sides. Place in shallow 2-quart baking pan; reserve drippings. Add lamb, onion, salt, and pepper to drippings. Cook until lamb is lightly browned. Place over eggplant. Add tomato sauce and Parmesan cheese. Bake in oven at 350° for 20 minutes. Add mozzarella cheese; bake 10 minutes or until cheese is bubbly and melted.

❋

Lamb Shanghai

Makes 4 to 6 servings

2 tablespoons butter
1½ pounds ground fresh lamb or the equivalent in finely chopped cooked lamb
1 pound mushrooms, sliced
3 cups chopped celery
¾ cup chopped celery tops

3 cups chopped onion
2 medium-sized green peppers, sliced
3 beef bouillon cubes
3 cups water
1 tablespoon soy sauce
½ cup all-purpose flour
Water
Cooked rice

Melt butter; add lamb and cook until lightly browned, stirring occasionally. Add mushrooms, celery, celery tops, onion, green peppers, bouillon cubes, 3 cups water, and soy sauce. Cook over low heat about 30 minutes or until vegetables are tender. Mix flour with a small amount of water; stir into lamb mixture. Cook, stirring constantly, until thickened. Serve with cooked rice.

❀

Stuffed Patties, Middle Eastern Style

Makes 6 servings

2 pounds ground lean lamb	3 hard-cooked eggs, sliced
2 tablespoons yogurt	¼ cup butter
1 tablespoon dry bread crumbs	1 cup finely chopped onion
2 cloves garlic, minced	1½ cups diced tomatoes
2½ teaspoons salt	1 tablespoon chopped parsley
½ teaspoon coriander	2 canned green chilies, chopped
¼ teaspoon ginger	½ teaspoon paprika
⅛ teaspoon cardamom	⅛ teaspoon turmeric
Dash turmeric	1½ cups bouillon or water
Dash cinnamon	
Dash cayenne pepper	

Combine lamb with next 10 ingredients; mix in electric mixer until fluffy. Shape into 12 patties, about ⅓ cup each. Place ½ sliced egg on each of six patties; top with remaining patties and seal edges. Brown stuffed patties on both sides in melted butter, about 10 minutes. Add onion and lightly brown. Mix in remaining ingredients. Simmer uncovered about 15 minutes or until patties are thoroughly cooked.

❀

Whole Leg, Rack, and Shoulder Lamb

Cuts for Roasting, Braising, or Boiling

Refer to time and temperature chart (p. 30) for instructions on preparing plain roasts.

Recipes in this section include those for cooking leg of lamb, boneless leg and shoulder, whole baby lamb, racks, and crown roast by dry-roasting or braising.

Boneless legs come rolled and tied or netted, and may weigh from 4½ to 6½ pounds, depending upon season and geographical source of the meat. Boneless shoulders also come rolled and tied or netted, and may weigh from 2¾ to 4¼ pounds, depending upon season and geographical source of meat.

Don't be afraid of large roasts. See section on "planover" dishes for ideas on use of leftovers. If your butcher sells only "long" legs containing the sirloin, and yours is not a large family, have the sirloin roast cut off for another meal, or slice sirloin into chops.

Whole baby lambs are not to be confused with "hothouse" lambs, which are six weeks to two months of age. Baby lambs are younger and smaller and must be obtained by special order.

A rack roast *is an uncut section of rib chops from one side or the other of the lamb carcass. A crown roast is made by bending two or more of these rib sections outward and sewing them together to form a crown.*

A square-cut shoulder roast *contains the blade and arm bones. The meat is delicious. It cannot be sliced, however, because of the bones, and must be "chunked" to serve, unless it is precarved. A cushion shoulder roast is a square-cut shoulder of lamb with the bones removed. Its sides are sewed together, with an opening for stuffing. After stuffing, the opening is skewered to close. A precarved shoulder roast is a square-cut shoulder roast which has been presliced on the band saw and tied back together with cord. The precarved shoulder roast is most popular when prepared with a sauce or glaze, or when braised. It can, however, be dry-roasted, but loses some of its moisture when cooked this way because of the precarving.*

Lamb Sauerbraten with Noodles

Makes 6 to 8 servings

2 cups vinegar
1 cup water
3 medium-sized onions, sliced
2 tablespoons sugar
½ teaspoon peppercorns
½ teaspoon whole cloves
4 bay leaves
1½ teaspoons dry mustard
8 teaspoons salt
4 pounds boneless lamb shoulder, rolled and tied
Flour, salt and pepper (for dredging)
¼ cup salad oil
⅓ cup gingersnap crumbs
4 to 6 quarts boiling water
1 pound (about 8 cups) medium egg noodles

Combine vinegar, 1 cup water, onions, sugar, peppercorns, cloves, bay leaves, mustard, and 2 teaspoons salt; mix well. Add meat. Cover and chill 2 to 4 days, turning meat each day. Drain meat; reserve vinegar mixture. Strain vinegar mixture. Dredge meat with flour, salt, and pepper. Cook in oil until browned on all sides. Add ¾ cup vinegar mixture. Cover and cook over low heat 3½ to 4 hours or until meat is tender. Remove meat; reserve ⅓ cup drippings. Combine ⅓ cup meat drippings and crumbs; blend. Gradually add remaining vinegar mixture and cook, stirring constantly, until thickened.

Meanwhile, add 2 tablespoons salt to rapidly boiling water. Gradually add noodles so that water continues to boil. Cook uncovered, stirring occasionally, until tender. Drain in colander. Serve noodles topped with meat and gravy.

❈

Lamb Shoulder on a Spit

Makes 6 servings

1 can (8 ounces) tomato sauce	¼ teaspoon pepper
1 teaspoon garlic salt	¼ cup molasses
1 teaspoon onion salt	1 boned shoulder of lamb (about 4 pounds), netted or rolled and tied
2 teaspoons Worcestershire sauce	

Combine tomato sauce, garlic salt, onion salt, Worcestershire sauce, pepper, and molasses; mix well. Place lamb on spit. Brush lamb with molasses mixture. Cook on rotisserie or on outdoor grill for 2½ to 3 hours or until meat thermometer registers 175° to 180°, depending upon desired degree of doneness. Brush lamb frequently with molasses mixture during cooking period.

❈

Lamb Shoulder Oriental

Makes 6 servings

1 medium-sized onion, chopped
¼ cup butter
3 cups soft bread crumbs
½ pound mushrooms, chopped
1 teaspoon salt
¼ teaspoon pepper
¼ teaspoon instant minced garlic
¼ teaspoon crushed rosemary
2 tablespoons sweet pickle relish
1 teaspoon soy sauce
1 egg
1 boned lamb shoulder (about 4 pounds), rolled and tied
Gravy (see below)

Sauté onion in butter until tender. Combine onion, bread crumbs, mushrooms, seasonings, pickle relish, soy sauce, and egg; mix thoroughly. Unroll lamb shoulder; mound stuffing in center of lamb; roll up and secure with string. Place on rack in shallow roasting pan; roast at 325° for 2½ hours. Drain off drippings, reserving 2 tablespoons for gravy. Place lamb on serving platter; make gravy in pan.

Gravy

Blend 3 tablespoons flour with 2 tablespoons lamb drippings in roasting pan; stir in 1¼ cups water, ½ teaspoon salt, dash pepper, and ½ teaspoon soy sauce. Cook, stirring constantly, until thickened. Strain gravy into serving dish.

Lamb à la Madeira

Makes 6 servings

1 teaspoon salt
¼ teaspoon pepper
½ teaspoon crushed basil
1 boned lamb shoulder
  (about 4 pounds),
  netted or rolled and tied
1 can (1 pound) purple
  plums

1 can (1 pound, 4½
  ounces) sliced pineapple
2 tablespoons cornstarch
Red food coloring
  (optional)
⅓ cup Madeira or orange
  juice

Mix salt, pepper, and basil; rub over lamb. Place lamb on rack in shallow roasting pan; roast at 325° for 2 hours. Drain syrup from plums and pineapple and stir into cornstarch in saucepan. Cook, stirring constantly, until glaze is thickened and clear. Add a few drops red food coloring, if desired. Drain off lamb drippings; pour 1 cup glaze over lamb, reserving remainder for sauce. Roast meat 30 to 60 minutes longer or until meat thermometer registers 175° to 180°, depending on desired degree of doneness. Baste occasionally with glaze from bottom of pan. Garnish lamb with pineapple and plums, and with parsley too, if desired. Stir wine and 2 tablespoons pan glaze into reserved glaze; heat and serve with lamb.

❂

Scandinavian Lamb Shoulder Roast

Makes 6 servings

¼ cup butter
1 boned shoulder of lamb (about 4 pounds), rolled and tied
1½ cups stock or bouillon
¼ cup sifted unbleached flour

¼ cup vinegar
⅓ cup chopped fresh dill or 1 teaspoon dry dill weed
1 teaspoon salt
¼ teaspoon pepper
Fresh dill for garnish

Melt butter in Dutch oven or kettle; add lamb and brown on all sides. Cover and cook slowly 3 hours or until tender, turning occasionally. Drain off drippings. Slowly stir stock or bouillon into flour; blend well. Add vinegar, ⅓ cup chopped dill, salt, and pepper; mix well. Pour dill mixture over lamb. Cover and cook over low heat about 30 minutes or until lamb is tender. Arrange lamb on serving platter; garnish with fresh dill, if available. Serve with dill sauce.

❂

Lamb Roast with Pineapple and Apricots

Makes 6 to 8 servings

1 boned shoulder of lamb (about 5 pounds), rolled and tied
Salt and pepper
1 can (1 pound, 4 ounces) sliced pineapple

1 can (1 pound, 13 ounces) whole apricots
1 teaspoon whole cloves
½ teaspoon nutmeg
¼ teaspoon allspice

Place lamb on rack in shallow roasting pan. Sprinkle with salt and pepper. Bake in slow (325°) oven 2 hours. Meanwhile, drain pineapple; reserve ½ cup pineapple syrup. Drain apricots; reserve ½ cup apricot syrup. Stud apricots with cloves. Combine pineapple syrup, apricot syrup, nutmeg, and allspice; mix well. Drain off lamb drippings. Arrange pineapple slices around lamb. Top with apricots. Pour fruit syrup mixture over lamb and fruit. Bake 30 minutes or until meat thermometer registers 175° to 180°, depending upon desired degree of doneness. Baste lamb and fruit with syrup mixture frequently during baking period.

❋

Lamb Shoulder with Almond Stuffing

Makes 6 servings

1 cup ground almonds	1 boned shoulder of lamb,
½ cup chopped dried	about 4 pounds
apricots	Salt and pepper

Combine almonds and apricots. Spread almond mixture on lamb. Roll up jelly-roll fashion. Fasten with string. Sprinkle with salt and pepper. Place on rack in shallow roasting pan. Roast in oven at 325° for 2½ to 3 hours or until meat thermometer registers 175° to 180°, depending upon desired degree of doneness.

❋

Agnellino al Forno (Roasted Baby Lamb)

1 baby spring lamb, about
7 to 12 pounds (allow ½
to ¾ pound per person,
minimum)
Salt
2 cloves garlic, slivered

½ cup lard
Pepper
4 whole cloves
2 whole apples
¼ cup sauterne or water

Have butcher clean lamb thoroughly, inside and out.
Wipe lamb with damp cloth, and sprinkle with salt inside
and out. Let stand for 15 minutes. Then, using a sharp
knife, make three parallel gashes about 2½ inches long
through the skin on each side of the backbone. Insert
slivers of garlic into each gash. Rub the whole lamb with
lard, and sprinkle with salt and pepper. Insert 2 cloves
in each apple, and place inside lamb. Sew cavity with
soft cord. Tie front legs forward and back legs backward,
so that lamb is trussed in kneeling position. Place in an
uncovered roasting pan, and roast in oven at 325° for
1 hour. Baste every 15 minutes with pan drippings. If lamb
is too dry, add wine or water. Prick the skin several times
during roasting with an icepick or fork so that it will not
blister. After 1 hour, turn the lamb, and raise the oven
temperature to 350° (if you like a crusty outside).
Continue to baste. Cook for another ½ hour, and turn
lamb again. Cook an additional ½ hour or until outside
is dark brown and crisp. Lamb should be done in 2½
to 4 hours depending upon size.

To serve, place on a large board, and garnish with sprigs
of parsley.

If you prefer moist, less browned lamb, roast at 325°
throughout and allow longer cooking time. Use of a meat
thermometer in the leg is recommended. Roast to an
internal temperature of 170° to 180°. Baby lamb requires

less roasting time per pound than other lamb. Normally about 20 minutes to the pound is sufficient.

NOTE: Baby lamb may also be roasted on a spit. Prepare in the same manner. Sprinkle inside and out with salt. But do not make gashes in skin; instead, put garlic inside body cavity with cloves and apples. Truss with wire, not cord. Roast until crisp and tender. An excellent outdoor treat. Hothouse lambs may be spit-roasted in the same manner.

❁

Cushion Shoulder of Lamb with Herbed Stuffing

Makes 6 to 8 servings

1 cushion-style lamb shoulder roast, 4 to 5 pounds
1 teaspoon salt
½ teaspoon pepper
2 tablespoons butter
1 cup diced celery
½ cup chopped onion
4 cups soft bread crumbs
2 tablespoons grated carrot
1½ teaspoons dehydrated mint leaves

Sprinkle lamb with ½ teaspoon salt and ¼ teaspoon pepper. Melt butter; add celery and onion; cook 5 minutes. Add bread crumbs, carrot, mint leaves, remaining ½ teaspoon salt, and remaining ¼ teaspoon pepper. Cook over low heat 10 minutes, stirring occasionally. Fill shoulder pocket with crumb mixture. Fasten with skewers. Place on rack in shallow roasting pan. Roast in oven at 325° for 2 to 2½ hours or until meat thermometer registers 175° to 180°, depending upon desired degree of doneness.

❁

Lamb Shoulder Roast with Spiced Pears

Makes 6 servings

1 can (1 pound, 13 ounces) pear halves
1 teaspoon whole cloves
¼ teaspoon mace
1 boned shoulder of lamb (about 4 pounds), rolled and tied or netted

Salt and pepper
2 tablespoons all-purpose flour
¼ teaspoon salt
1½ cups water

Drain pears; reserve syrup. Stud pears with cloves. Combine 1 cup pear syrup and mace; mix well. Pour over pears. Chill 2½ hours. Drain.

Meanwhile, place lamb on rack in roasting pan. Sprinkle with salt and pepper. Roast in oven at 325° for 2½ hours. Pour remaining pear syrup over lamb. Roast 30 minutes, or until meat thermometer registers 175° to 180°, depending upon desired degree of doneness. Baste frequently during roasting period. Remove lamb to heated platter. Combine flour, ¼ teaspoon salt and water; blend. Add to lamb drippings. Cook until thickened, stirring constantly. Serve gravy and pears with lamb.

❁

French Marinated Leg of Lamb

Makes 6 to 8 servings

1 cup French dressing
2 small onions, sliced
2 cloves garlic, slivered

1 teaspoon ginger
1 leg of lamb, 4 to 5 pounds

Mix together French dressing, onions, garlic, and ginger; pour over lamb. Chill six hours or overnight, turning occasionally. Drain lamb, reserving marinade; place meat on rack in shallow roasting pan. Roast in oven at 325° for 2½ hours or until meat thermometer registers 175° to 180°, depending upon desired degree of doneness. Baste occasionally with marinade.

❁

Marinated Barbecued Lamb

Makes 6 to 8 servings

1 medium-sized green pepper, diced	1 teaspoon pepper
	⅛ teaspoon marjoram
2 medium-sized tomatoes, diced	⅛ teaspoon dry mustard
	⅛ teaspoon Tabasco
1 medium-sized onion, sliced	1 cup port
	1 cup water
½ cup coarsely chopped parsley	½ cup olive or salad oil
3 cloves garlic, minced	1 boned leg or shoulder of lamb (about 6 pounds), rolled and tied
1 tablespoon salt	

In large shallow pan, mix together vegetables, seasonings, wine, water, and oil. Add lamb; cover and chill 1 day, turning lamb occasionally. Drain vegetables, reserving both marinade and vegetables. Place lamb on spit; cook in rotisserie or on outdoor grill 2½ hours (or allow 30 to 35 minutes per pound) or until meat thermometer registers 175° to 180°, depending upon desired degree of doneness. Brush lamb frequently with marinade while cooking. Serve with marinated vegetables.

❁

Anchovy Lamb Shoulder

Makes 6 servings

1 boned shoulder of lamb
(about 4 pounds), rolled
and tied
Salt and pepper
2 cans (2 ounces each) flat
anchovies

½ cup melted butter
3 tablespoons lemon juice
8 small onions, cooked
8 medium-sized
mushrooms

Sprinkle lamb with salt and pepper. Place on rack in roasting
pan. Roast in oven at 325° for 1½ hours. Drain off
drippings. Drain anchovies; reserve oil. Finely chop
anchovies. Combine anchovies, reserved anchovy oil, butter
and lemon juice; mix well. Spoon half of anchovy mixture
over lamb. Roast 1 hour. Arrange onions and mushrooms on
eight small skewers and arrange on lamb. Brush mushrooms
and onions with anchovy mixture. Roast ½ to 1 hour or
until meat thermometer registers 175° to 180°, depending
on desired degree of doneness. Baste lamb with anchovy
mixture frequently during cooking period.

❁

Pineapple-Chutney Lamb Shoulder

Makes 6 servings

1 boned shoulder of lamb
(about 4 pounds), rolled
and tied
Salt to taste
1 can (1 pound, 4 ounces)
crushed pineapple

¼ cup firmly packed
brown sugar
½ cup chutney
1 teaspoon ginger
1 teaspoon salt
¼ cup butter

Sprinkle lamb with salt to taste. Place on rack in roasting pan. Roast at 325° for 1½ hours. Drain off drippings. Combine remaining ingredients and cook over medium heat to boiling point. Cook 5 minutes over low heat, stirring occasionally. Spoon ⅓ of pineapple mixture over lamb. Roast 1½ to 2 hours or until meat thermometer registers 175° to 180°, depending upon desired degree of doneness. Baste lamb with remaining pineapple mixture frequently during cooking period.

❁

Barbecued Lamb Roast

Makes 6 servings

1 boned shoulder of lamb (about 4 pounds), rolled and tied
1 teaspoon whole cloves
¼ cup salad oil
2 tablespoons dill-pickle liquid
⅓ cup firmly packed brown sugar
¼ cup finely chopped dill pickles
1 teaspoon salt
½ teaspoon allspice

Stud lamb with cloves. Place lamb on spit. Cook in rotisserie or on outdoor grill about 2½ to 3 hours or until meat thermometer registers 175° to 180°, depending upon desired degree of doneness. Combine remaining ingredients; stir and heat to boiling point. Baste lamb frequently with sauce while cooking.

❁

Barbecued Baked Shoulder of Lamb

Makes 6 servings

1 boned shoulder of lamb (about 4 pounds), rolled and tied or netted
Salt and pepper to taste
1 clove garlic, slivered
3 tablespoons olive oil
1 cup finely chopped onion
1 can (8 ounces) tomato sauce
1 can (6 ounces) tomato paste
1 teaspoon dry mustard
1 teaspoon Worcestershire sauce
2 tablespoons brown sugar
¼ cup vinegar
1 teaspoon salt
¼ teaspoon pepper

Sprinkle lamb with salt and pepper to taste. Stud lamb with slivered garlic. Place lamb on rack in shallow roasting pan. Roast in oven at 325° for 2½ hours.

Meanwhile, heat oil; add onion and cook over low heat until tender. Add remaining ingredients; mix. Cook 30 minutes over low heat, stirring occasionally. Pour over lamb. Roast 30 minutes or until meat thermometer registers 175° to 180°, depending upon desired degree of doneness. Baste with barbecue sauce frequently during baking period.

❁

Spicy Lamb Shoulder with Apples

Makes about 6 servings

2 teaspoons salt
¼ teaspoon pepper
1½ teaspoons ginger
½ teaspoon nutmeg
¾ teaspoon cinnamon
1 boned shoulder of lamb (about 4 pounds), rolled and tied or netted
½ cup honey
2 medium-sized apples, cored and cut in wedges

Combine salt, pepper, 1 teaspoon ginger, ¼ teaspoon nutmeg, and ½ teaspoon cinnamon; mix. Rub salt mixture over lamb. Place lamb on rack in shallow roasting pan. Roast in oven at 325° for approximately 2½ hours or until meat thermometer registers 175° to 180°, depending upon desired degree of doneness. Combine remaining ½ teaspoon ginger, ¼ teaspoon nutmeg, and ¼ teaspoon cinnamon with honey; mix well. Add apples and cook 10 minutes over low heat. Serve lamb with apple-honey mixture.

❄

Festive Shoulder of Lamb (Rolled or Netted)

Makes 6 servings

1 boned shoulder of lamb (about 4 pounds), rolled and tied or netted	Salt and pepper
	¾ cup orange juice
	3 tablespoons mint jelly
1 teaspoon thyme	6 canned pear halves
½ teaspoon basil	

Place lamb on rack in roasting pan. Sprinkle with thyme, basil, and salt and pepper. Roast in oven at 325° for 2¼ hours. Pour orange juice over lamb. Roast 30 minutes or until meat thermometer registers 175° to 180°, depending upon desired degree of doneness. Baste lamb with drippings during roasting period. Place 1½ teaspoons mint jelly in each pear half. Garnish shoulder of lamb with pear halves.

❄

Rice-Stuffed Cushion Lamb Shoulder

Makes 6 servings

2 cups cooked rice
1½ teaspoons salt
¼ teaspoon pepper
1 medium-sized onion, finely chopped
1 medium-sized green pepper, finely chopped
¼ teaspoon saffron (optional)
1 cushion-style lamb shoulder roast, 4 to 5 pounds

Combine rice, salt, pepper, onion, green pepper, and saffron; mix well. Fill lamb cushion with rice mixture. Fasten with skewers. Place lamb on rack in shallow roasting pan. Roast in oven at 325° for 2½ to 3 hours or until meat thermometer registers 175° to 180°, depending upon desired degree of doneness.

❋

Leg of Lamb Neapolitan

Makes 8 to 10 servings

1 leg of lamb, about 6 pounds
2 teaspoons salt
1 teaspoon crushed oregano
4 medium-sized onions, chopped
1 medium-sized green pepper, chopped
1 clove garlic, crushed
1 can (1 pound, 12 ounces) tomatoes

Sprinkle lamb with salt and oregano; place on rack in shallow roasting pan. Roast in oven at 325° for 1½ hours; drain off drippings. Mix together the onions, green pepper, garlic, and tomatoes. Baste lamb with some of the tomato mixture, and roast, basting occasionally, 1 hour or until meat thermometer registers 175° to 180°, depending upon desired degree of doneness. Add water to sauce if needed during latter part of cooking time. Serve roast with sauce.

❀

Lamb Barbacoa

Makes 8 to 10 servings

1 medium-sized green pepper, diced

2 medium-sized tomatoes, diced

1 medium-sized onion, sliced

½ cup coarsely chopped parsley

3 cloves garlic, minced

1 tablespoon salt

1 teaspoon pepper

⅛ teaspoon each: marjoram, dry mustard, Tabasco

2 tablespoons red wine vinegar*

1¾ cups water

½ cup olive or salad oil

1 leg of lamb (about 5 to 6 pounds), boned, rolled and tied or netted

In advance: In large shallow pan, combine vegetables with seasonings, vinegar, water, and oil. Add lamb; cover and chill one day, turning occasionally.

At cooking time: Drain and reserve vegetables and marinade. Secure lamb on spit. Cook on rotisserie or on outdoor grill 2½ to 3 hours or until meat thermometer registers 175° to 180°, depending on desired degree of doneness, basting frequently with marinade. Serve with marinated vegetables.

* Or use 1 cup port and eliminate ¾ cup of the water.

❀

Apricot-Glazed Rolled Shoulder of Lamb

Makes 6 servings

1 boned shoulder of lamb
(about 4 pounds), rolled
and tied or netted
Salt and pepper to taste

1 can (1 pound, 13 ounces)
apricot halves
1 cup firmly packed brown
sugar
1 teaspoon nutmeg

Sprinkle lamb with salt and pepper to taste. Place on rack in shallow roasting pan. Roast in oven at 325° for 2½ hours.

Meanwhile, drain apricots; reserve syrup. Force apricots through food mill or sieve. Combine apricots, apricot syrup, brown sugar, and nutmeg; mix well. Pour apricot mixture over lamb. Roast 30 minutes longer or until meat thermometer registers 175° to 180°, depending upon desired degree of doneness. Baste lamb with apricot mixture frequently during cooking period.

❂

Holiday Lamb Roast

Makes 6 to 8 servings

2 beef-bouillon cubes
1 cup boiling water
¼ cup chopped onion
½ teaspoon salt
¼ teaspoon pepper
2 cups cooked brown rice
¼ cup blanched slivered
almonds

¼ cup chopped dried
apricots
¼ cup chopped dried figs
¼ cup chopped pitted
dates
1 tablespoon raisins
1 cushion-style lamb
shoulder roast, 4 to 5
pounds

Dissolve bouillon cubes in boiling water; add onion, salt, pepper, rice, almonds, and fruit. Fill lamb pocket with fruit-rice stuffing; truss with string or skewers. Place lamb on rack in roasting pan. Roast in oven at 325° for 2½ to 3 hours or until desired degree of doneness.

❄

Leg of Lamb, French Style

Makes 6 to 8 servings

4 cloves garlic
1 leg of lamb, about 5 pounds
1 cup water
1 cup dry red wine
1 cup chopped onion
2 tablespoons cornstarch
1 can (1 pound) red kidney beans

Insert garlic in lamb. Place lamb on rack in shallow roasting pan. Combine water and wine. Pour over lamb. Roast in oven at 325° for 3 hours. Baste with wine mixture frequently during cooking period. Drain off and reserve drippings. Roast lamb 30 minutes or until meat thermometer registers 175° to 180°, depending upon desired degree of doneness.

Meanwhile, cook onion in drippings 10 minutes. Blend in cornstarch and add beans. Cook over medium heat until thickened and clear, stirring constantly. Serve bean mixture with lamb.

❄

Leg of Lamb with Coffee Gravy & Orange Cups

Makes 6 to 8 servings

2 cups coffee
¼ teaspoon allspice
½ teaspoon cinnamon
⅔ cup honey
1 leg of lamb, about 5 pounds
3 large oranges

⅓ cup chopped maraschino cherries, about 15 cherries
4 teaspoons all-purpose flour
¼ cup water
Fresh mint sprigs
⅓ cup brandy

Combine coffee, allspice, cinnamon, and honey; mix well. Place lamb on rack in shallow roasting pan. Roast in oven at 325° for 2½ to 3 hours or until meat thermometer registers 175° to 180°, depending upon desired degree of doneness. Baste lamb with coffee mixture frequently during cooking period.

Meanwhile, cut oranges in half crosswise. Scoop out pulp; reserve shells. Chop orange pulp and combine with cherries. Spoon into orange shells. Arrange around lamb during last 20 minutes of cooking period.

Remove lamb and orange cups from roasting pan; reserve drippings. Combine flour and water; mix well. Blend flour mixture into drippings in pan. Cook over low heat, stirring constantly, until thickened. Arrange lamb and orange cups on platter. Garnish with mint, as desired. Heat brandy; pour over orange cups. Ignite. Serve lamb and orange cups with coffee gravy. Serve immediately.

❊

Holiday Lamb Roast with Fruit

Makes 6 servings

1 boneless shoulder of
    lamb (about 4 pounds),
    rolled and tied or netted
Salt and pepper
2 tablespoons honey

2 tablespoons butter
1 tablespoon lemon juice
1 can (1 pound, 4 ounces)
    pear halves, drained
¾ cup grapes, pitted

Place lamb on rack in roasting pan. Sprinkle with salt
and pepper. Roast in oven at 325° for 2 hours. Drain off
drippings. Combine honey, butter, and lemon juice. Cook
over low heat until butter melts. Arrange pears around
lamb. Arrange grapes in center of pears. Pour honey
mixture over fruit. Roast about 30 minutes or until meat
thermometer registers 175° to 180°, depending upon
desired degree of doneness.

❂

Onion-Orange Lamb Roast

Makes 8 servings

1 leg of lamb, about 5
    pounds
¼ cup chopped onion
½ cup orange juice

2 tablespoons prepared
    mustard
¾ teaspoon rosemary
Salt and pepper

Place lamb on rack in roasting pan. Roast in oven at 325°
for 2 hours. Combine onion, orange juice, mustard, and
rosemary; mix well. Pour over lamb. Sprinkle with salt
and pepper. Roast 1 to 2 hours or until meat thermometer
registers 175° to 180°, depending upon desired degree of
doneness.

❂

Roast Lamb with Currant Orange Sauce

Makes 8 servings

1 leg of lamb, about 5 pounds
½ teaspoon rosemary
1 jar (12 ounces) currant jelly

½ cup canned pineapple juice
1 jar (10 ounces) mandarin orange sections

Place lamb on rack in roasting pan. Sprinkle with rosemary. Roast in oven at 325° for 2½ hours. Drain off drippings. Add currant jelly, pineapple juice, and undrained orange sections. Roast 30 minutes to 1 hour or until meat thermometer registers 175° to 180°, depending upon desired degree of doneness.

❁

Italian Leg of Lamb

Makes 8 servings

1 leg of lamb, about 5 pounds
Salt
4 medium-sized onions, chopped
1 medium-sized green pepper, chopped
1 clove garlic, finely chopped

2 cans (1 pound each) tomatoes
1 medium-sized chili pepper, chopped (optional)
1 tablespoon salt
3 quarts boiling water
8 ounces spaghetti
Grated Parmesan cheese

Place lamb on rack in shallow roasting pan. Sprinkle with salt. Roast in oven at 325° for 1 hour. Combine onions, green pepper, garlic, undrained tomatoes, and chili pepper;

mix well. Pour over lamb. Roast 2 to 3 hours or until meat thermometer registers 175° to 180°, depending upon desired degree of doneness. Baste lamb frequently during roasting period.

Meanwhile, add 1 tablespoon salt to rapidly boiling water. Gradually add spaghetti so that water continues to boil. Cook uncovered, stirring occasionally, until tender. Drain in colander. Place lamb on serving platter. Top spaghetti with tomato mixture. Serve Parmesan cheese with spaghetti.

❁

Crown Roast of Lamb with Olive Stuffing

Makes 6 servings

2 pounds ground lamb
⅓ cup finely chopped pimiento-stuffed green olives
1 medium-sized onion, chopped
1 cup fine dry bread crumbs
2 eggs, beaten
½ cup milk

⅛ teaspoon thyme
¼ teaspoon basil
Salt to taste
¼ teaspoon pepper
1 crown roast of lamb (5 to 6 pounds), containing 2 whole rib sections; allow 2 rib sections per serving

Combine ground lamb, olives, onion, bread crumbs, eggs, milk, thyme, basil, salt, and pepper; mix well. Fill roast with lamb stuffing. Place on rack in shallow roasting pan. Roast in oven at 325° for 2½ hours or until meat thermometer registers 175° to 180°, depending upon desired degree of doneness. Garnish with whole cooked white onions, sliced olives, and parsley, as desired.

❁

Roast Leg of Lamb, Brussels Sprouts, & Baby Carrots, au Vin Blanc

Makes 6 servings

1 leg of lamb, about 5
pounds
½ teaspoon salt
1 cup currant jelly
2 packages (10 ounces
each) frozen Brussels
sprouts

½ cup dry white wine
1 can (1 pound) whole
small carrots, drained
Salt and pepper to taste

Sprinkle lamb with ½ teaspoon salt. Place on rack in shallow roasting pan. Roast in slow (325°) oven about 2½ hours or until meat thermometer registers 175° to 180°, depending upon desired degree of doneness. At the end of 1 hour, spread lamb with currant jelly; continue roasting, brushing frequently with the jelly. During last 45 minutes of roasting, arrange frozen Brussels sprouts around lamb and baste with some of the wine. During the last 15 minutes of roasting, arrange carrots around lamb and baste with remaining wine. Season vegetables with salt and pepper.

❖

Leg of Lamb with Peaches & Pears

Makes 8 to 10 servings

1 leg of lamb, 5 to 6
pounds
Salt and pepper
1 can (1 pound) pear
halves, drained

1 teaspoon whole cloves
1 package (12 ounces)
frozen sliced peaches,
thawed

Place lamb on rack in roasting pan. Sprinkle lamb with salt and pepper. Roast in oven at 325° for 2½ hours. Drain off drippings.

Meanwhile, stud pears with cloves. Arrange pears around lamb. Pour undrained peaches over lamb and pears. Roast 30 minutes or until meat thermometer registers 175° to 180°, depending upon desired degree of doneness. Baste lamb with peach mixture frequently during cooking period.

❋

Vegetable-Stuffed Crown Roast of Lamb

Makes 6 to 8 servings

1 cup water
½ cup butter
1 package (8 ounces) bread-stuffing mix
1 teaspoon salt
¼ teaspoon pepper
1 egg, slightly beaten
1 cup chopped celery
1 cup grated carrots

1 medium-sized onion, chopped
1 medium-sized green pepper, chopped
1 crown roast of lamb (5 to 6 pounds), containing 2 whole rib sections; allow 2 rib portions per serving

Combine water and butter and heat to boiling point. Add stuffing mix, salt, pepper, egg, celery, carrots, onion, and green pepper; mix well. Place lamb on rack in shallow roasting pan. Fill with vegetable-stuffing mixture. Roast in oven at 325° for 2 to 2½ hours or until meat thermometer registers 175° to 180°, depending upon desired degree of doneness. Serve with lamb gravy, if desired.

❋

Special Lamb Roast

Makes 10 to 12 servings

1 leg of lamb, 6 to 8 pounds	1 teaspoon thyme
	½ teaspoon basil
1½ cups fine dry bread crumbs	1 teaspoon salt
	¼ teaspoon pepper

Place lamb on rack in roasting pan. Roast in oven at 325° for 3 hours. Combine remaining ingredients; mix well. Spread over lamb. Roast 30 minutes to 1 hour or until meat thermometer registers 175° to 180°, depending upon desired degree of doneness.

❂

Pineapple-Glazed Leg of Lamb

Makes 8 servings

1 leg of lamb, about 5 pounds	½ cup molasses
	1 teaspoon salt
1 can (1 pound, 4 ounces) pineapple chunks	¼ teaspoon pepper

Place lamb on rack in shallow roasting pan. Roast in oven at 325° for 1 hour. Combine undrained pineapple with remaining ingredients; mix well. Pour over lamb. Roast 1½ to 2 hours or until meat thermometer registers 175° to 180°, depending upon desired degree of doneness. Baste frequently during roasting period.

❂

Kharoff (Stuffed Crown Roast)

Makes 6 to 7 servings

- 1 pound lean lamb, cut in small cubes
- 1 medium-sized onion, chopped
- 1 cup water
- 1 teaspoon salt
- ¼ teaspoon pepper
- ¼ teaspoon cinnamon
- ¼ teaspoon cardamom
- ¼ teaspoon powdered cloves
- ¼ teaspoon ginger
- 2 cups cooked rice
- ¼ cup raisins
- ¼ cup toasted slivered almonds
- 1 crown roast of lamb (5 to 6 pounds), containing 2 whole rib sections; allow at least 2 ribs per serving
- 3 hard-cooked eggs

In saucepan, slowly cook lamb cubes and onion in water, covered, until liquid is reduced to about ¼ cup (about 20 minutes). Mix together seasonings, rice, raisins, and almonds (save some almonds for garnish). Add meat mixture and toss lightly.

Place roast on rack in shallow roasting pan. Half-fill with stuffing. Cut 2 hard-cooked eggs in quarters lengthwise and arrange on stuffing. Add remaining stuffing. Cover top of roast and stuffing with aluminum foil. Roast in oven at 325° for 2½ hours or until meat thermometer registers 175° for medium doneness. Uncover during the last 15 minutes of roasting time. Garnish with remaining egg, sliced, and reserved almonds. Add parsley sprigs, if desired.

❈

Crown Roast of Lamb

Makes 6 to 7 servings

- 2 pounds ground lamb
- 1 medium-sized green pepper, finely chopped
- 2/3 cup chopped onion
- 3/4 cup fine dry bread crumbs
- 1 can (3 ounces) sliced mushrooms
- 2 eggs, beaten
- 2 teaspoons salt
- 1/4 teaspoon pepper
- 1 crown roast of lamb (5 to 6 pounds), containing 2 whole rib sections; allow 2 rib portions per serving
- Salt and pepper to taste

Combine ground lamb, green pepper, onion, bread crumbs, undrained mushrooms, eggs, 2 teaspoons salt, and 1/4 teaspoon pepper; mix well. Sprinkle crown roast with salt and pepper to taste. Fill crown roast with stuffing mixture. Place on rack in shallow roasting pan. Roast in oven at 325° for 2½ hours or until meat thermometer registers 175° to 180°, depending upon desired degree of doneness. Garnish with large pimiento-stuffed green olives and serve with mint jelly, as desired.

❖

Rack of Lamb with Matzo Dressing

Makes 4 servings

- 1 French rack of lamb, about 3 pounds (allow 2 ribs per serving)
- Salt and pepper to taste
- 3 cups boiling water
- 6 cups coarsely broken matzos
- 1/4 cup salad oil
- 2 medium-sized onions, sliced
- 1/2 cup chopped celery
- 1/4 cup chopped parsley
- 2 eggs, beaten
- Parsley
- Hard-cooked egg slices

Sprinkle lamb with salt and pepper to taste. Place lamb on rack in shallow roasting pan. Roast in oven at 325° for 1 hour.

Meanwhile, pour water over matzos; let stand until water is absorbed. Heat oil. Add onions and celery and cook until lightly browned. Combine matzos and additional salt and pepper to taste; add to onion mixture and cook 5 minutes or until matzo mixture is browned, stirring occasionally. Stir 1/4 cup chopped parsley and matzo mixture into eggs. Turn into lightly oiled casserole. Bake lamb and matzo dressing 30 minutes or until meat thermometer registers 175° to 180°, depending upon desired degree of doneness. Garnish with parsley and egg slices.

❁

Lamb with Lemon Glaze

Makes 6 to 8 servings

1 leg of lamb, about 5 pounds	1 teaspoon sugar
	3/4 cup water
1 tablespoon cornstarch	1/4 cup lemon juice
1 clove garlic, crushed	

Place lamb on rack in shallow roasting pan. Bake in slow (325°) oven 2 1/2 hours. Drain off drippings. Combine cornstarch, garlic, and sugar; blend. Gradually add water and cook over low heat, stirring constantly until thickened and clear. Add lemon juice; mix well. Pour lemon mixture over lamb. Bake 30 to 60 minutes or until meat thermometer registers 175° to 180°, depending upon desired degree of doneness. Baste lamb with lemon mixture frequently during cooking period.

❁

Lamb Kebabs

❦❦❦❦❦❦❦ ❦❦❦❦❦❦❦❦ ❦❦❦❦

Enjoyment of lamb prepared in the form of kebabs is perhaps the oldest lamb-eating custom we know. The nomads of the Middle East prepared lamb meat this way over their campfires. Warriors skewered the meat on their swords. There is still no tastier way to prepare lamb—indoors or out. Many cuts of lamb can be skewered and roasted over coals satisfactorily—cubes from shoulder or leg, rib racks, chops, and sirloin steaks. You will find that lamb is compatible with fruits or vegetables and may be marinated or not, as you wish. Don't be afraid to experiment with new combinations of flavors. The ideas in this section provide only the beginning. Fruits are especially good with lamb. In using fruits or vegetables, however, just remember that they cook more quickly than meat. So it is a good idea to skewer them separately instead of alternating them with lamb on the same skewer. Vegetables which can be alternated with smaller lamb cubes and which hold up satisfactorily are green-pepper squares, small whole onions, and cherry tomatoes. Pickles, stuffed olives, kumquats, and the firmer vegetables, such as cauliflower and cooked carrots, may also be used.

Outdoor Lamb Kebabs

Makes 6 servings

2 pounds lamb shoulder
   or leg, cubed
12 small whole onions,
   cooked
6 cherry tomatoes
12 large pimiento-stuffed
   olives

Salt and pepper
½ cup vinegar
½ teaspoon soy sauce
¼ teaspoon dry mustard
3 tablespoons sugar

Alternate lamb cubes and vegetables on skewers. Sprinkle
with salt and pepper. Combine vinegar, soy sauce, mustard,
and sugar. Brush kebabs with half of the vinegar mixture.
Broil 3 to 4 inches from source of heat, or cook on outdoor
grill 5 to 7 minutes or to desired degree of doneness.
Brush with remaining vinegar mixture. Turn kebabs
frequently during cooking period.

❋

Armenian Shish Kebab

Makes 4 servings

¼ cup olive oil
¼ cup lemon juice
1½ teaspoons ginger
1 teaspoon coriander
1 clove garlic, crushed
½ teaspoon curry powder
1 teaspoon salt

1 teaspoon garlic salt
1 pound lamb shoulder, cut
   into 2-inch cubes
8 small tomatoes
2 medium-sized green
   peppers, cut into 2½-
   inch squares

Combine olive oil, lemon juice, ginger, coriander, garlic,
curry powder, salt, and garlic salt; mix well. Add lamb.
Chill 2 to 3 hours, turning lamb occasionally. Arrange

lamb on four skewers. Reserve olive-oil mixture. Broil lamb, 3 to 4 inches from source of heat, or cook on grill 5 to 7 minutes. Turn. Place tomatoes and green peppers alternately on skewers. Brush lamb and vegetable kebabs with remaining olive-oil mixture. Cook 5 minutes longer or until lamb is desired degree of doneness.

❁

Lamb Rib Racks en Brochette

Makes 6 servings

1 cup salad oil
½ cup cider vinegar
¼ cup water
¼ cup sugar
1 tablespoon soy sauce
2 pieces (about 1 inch each) dry ginger root
1 clove garlic, crushed
6 (3 bones thick) lamb rib chops

3 slices (⅓ inch thick) fresh pineapple, cut into 4 wedges
1 large green pepper, cut into 12 pieces
1 can (5 ounces) water chestnuts, drained
Red maraschino cherries (optional)

Combine oil, vinegar, water, sugar, soy sauce, ginger, and garlic. Pour over remaining ingredients. Marinate several hours, turning occasionally. Place lamb on spit; cook 30 minutes or until desired doneness, brushing frequently with marinade. Skewer pineapple, pepper, water chestnuts (use twisting motion to avoid splitting), and cherries. Grill about 10 minutes or until done, brushing frequently with marinade.

❁

Kalypso Kebabs

Makes 4 servings

1 pound lamb shoulder, diced
1 can (1 pound, 13 ounces) peach halves
4 medium-sized bananas, cut in 1-inch slices
1 package (8 ounces) pitted dates
24 (about ½ cup) red maraschino cherries
2 tablespoons melted butter
1 tablespoon lemon juice
1 teaspoon cinnamon
¼ teaspoon powdered cloves

Arrange lamb on skewers. Drain peaches, reserving syrup. Coat banana slices with syrup. Arrange peach half, 3 dates, 3 banana slices, and 3 cherries on each of eight skewers. Combine melted butter, lemon juice, cinnamon, and cloves for basting sauce. Broil lamb, 3 to 4 inches from source of heat, or cook on outdoor grill 5 to 7 minutes; turn. Add fruit skewers; brush with basting sauce, cook 5 to 7 minutes longer, turning fruit skewers once; brush with sauce frequently.

❁

Shish Kebab Casserole

Makes 4 servings

4 large mushrooms
1 cup uncooked rice
3 cups stock or bouillon
2 tablespoons vinegar
1 teaspoon salt
½ teaspoon basil
⅛ teaspoon pepper
2 cups shoulder of lamb, cut into 1½-inch cubes
1 cup small white onions
1 medium-sized green pepper, diced

Remove stems from mushrooms; chop stems. Combine mushroom stems, rice, stock or bouillon, vinegar, salt, basil, and pepper; mix well. Turn into shallow 2-quart casserole. Arrange mushroom caps and remaining ingredients on skewers. Arrange on rice mixture. Bake in preheated oven at 350° for 1 hour.

❉

Souvlakia

Makes 4 servings

4 ounces sweetbreads or additional ½ pound meat	¼ cup lemon juice
	2 tablespoons wine vinegar
1 pound boned leg of lamb, cut into 2-inch cubes	1 tablespoon oregano
	1 teaspoon salt
¼ cup olive oil	¼ teaspoon pepper
	2 cloves garlic, chopped
½ cup dry white wine	1 small onion, chopped

Cut sweetbreads in 8 pieces. Using four 8-inch stainless-steel skewers, arrange the meat, alternating kinds. In a flat pan, combine remaining ingredients to make a marinade. Soak the meat in this, refrigerated, at least 12 hours. Turn it occasionally.

Place the skewered meat on broiler pan; place on farthest rack from flame, and broil for 50 minutes. Baste with the marinade and turn every 15 minutes. This dish can also be cooked on an outdoor rotisserie with meat arranged on one large spit. If this is done, keep heat low and allow two hours' cooking time. Baste often.

❉

Lamb & Fruit Kebabs

Makes 4 servings

1½ pounds leg or shoulder of lamb, cut into 2-inch cubes

1 small pineapple, pared, cored, and cut into 10 wedges

1 large apple, cored and quartered

12 preserved kumquats

¼ cup maraschino cherries, about 10 cherries

¼ cup butter, melted

½ teaspoon seasoned salt

½ teaspoon paprika

Arrange lamb, pineapple, apple, kumquats, and cherries on skewers. Combine butter, salt, and paprika; blend. Brush fruits with butter mixture. Broil, 4 to 5 inches from source of heat, or cook on outdoor grill 12 to 15 minutes or until lamb is desired degree of doneness. Brush fruits with butter mixture during cooking period. Turn kebabs frequently during cooking period.

❀

Barbecued Lamb Kebabs

Makes 4 to 6 servings

1½ pounds leg or shoulder of lamb, cut into 2-inch cubes

2 medium-sized zucchini, sliced

1½ cups cauliflower, broken into florets

12 small carrots, cooked

12 small potatoes, cooked

Paprika

6 tablespoons chili sauce

1 tablespoon prepared mustard

3 tablespoons salad oil

Arrange lamb, zucchini, carrots, and cauliflower on skewers. Sprinkle potatoes with paprika. Combine remaining ingredients; mix well. Brush with sauce. Broil, 4 to 5 inches from source of heat, or cook on outdoor grill 12 to 15 minutes or until lamb is desired degree of doneness. Brush with oil mixture during cooking period. Turn kebabs frequently during cooking period.

❈

Chili-Flavored Shish Kebab

Makes 6 servings

⅓ cup lemon juice
¼ cup salad oil
1 clove garlic, finely chopped
½ teaspoon chili powder
½ teaspoon ginger
½ teaspoon salt
1½ pounds boneless lamb shoulder, cut in 1½-inch cubes

1 cup cauliflower, broken into florets and cooked
2 medium-sized tomatoes, cut in wedges (skewered through the skin) or 12 cherry tomatoes

Combine lemon juice, oil, garlic, chili powder, ginger, and salt; mix well. Add lamb. Cover and chill several hours, stirring occasionally. Drain; reserve marinade. Arrange lamb, cauliflower, and tomato wedges on skewers. Brush with marinade. Broil, 3 to 4 inches from source of heat, 5 to 7 minutes or until lightly browned on all sides. Brush with marinade frequently during broiling period.

❈

Curried Lamb Kebabs

Makes 8 servings

- 1 cup apple sauce
- 1 tablespoon curry powder
- 1 teaspoon salt
- ¼ teaspoon pepper
- 2 tablespoons lemon juice
- 2 pounds lamb shoulder, diced

Combine apple sauce, curry powder, salt, pepper, and lemon juice; mix well. Add lamb and stir. Chill two hours. Arrange lamb on skewers. Broil lamb, 3 to 4 inches from source of heat, 5 to 7 minutes on each side or until desired degree of doneness.

❂

Burgundy Lamb Kebabs

Makes 4 servings

- 2 tablespoons olive or salad oil
- ⅓ cup burgundy
- ½ teaspoon tarragon
- 1 teaspoon salt
- ¼ teaspoon pepper
- ½ teaspoon oregano
- 1 pound shoulder of lamb, cut into 1½-inch cubes

Combine oil, wine, tarragon, salt, pepper, and oregano; mix well. Add lamb and chill 3 hours, turning lamb occasionally. Remove lamb and reserve wine mixture. Arrange lamb on four skewers and brush with wine mixture. Broil, 4 to 5 inches from source of heat, 5 to 7 minutes. Turn lamb and brush with remaining wine mixture. Broil 5 to 7 minutes or until lamb is desired degree of doneness.

❂

Indonesian Lamb Sate

Makes 6 servings

2 medium-sized onions, finely chopped

1 or 2 cloves garlic, minced

¼ cup smooth peanut butter

2 tablespoons brown sugar

¼ teaspoon salt

¼ teaspoon crushed red pepper

¼ cup soy sauce

3 tablespoons lemon juice

2 pounds boned leg of lamb, cut into 1-inch cubes

Mix together all ingredients in bowl except lamb. Add lamb; chill overnight. Skewer meat; reserve marinade. Broil lamb, 3 inches from source of heat, 10 minutes on each side, brushing occasionally with marinade.

❈

Lamb Chops
and Steaks

❧❧❧❧❧❧❧❧ ❧❧❧❧❧❧❧❧ ❧❧❧❧

*Refer to time and temperature chart (p. 30) for
instructions on broiling, pan-broiling, frying, or braising
plain chops and steaks.*

*Recipes in this section apply to rib chops, loin chops,
sirloin chops, round-bone or blade-bone shoulder chops,
Scotch chops and leg steaks. (The terms "chop" and
"steak" are used interchangeably in referring to slices
from the sirloin and from the round-bone and blade-bone
sides of the shoulder.)*

ENGLISH CHOPS *are double loin chops cut across the
carcass. They are also sometimes boned and skewered into
a round chop surrounded by a narrow strip of fat.*

SARATOGA CHOPS *are made from the inside shoulder
muscle, which is the continuing eye of the rack or rib
section. They, too, are round and boneless.*

FRENCH CHOPS *are rib chops with the meat trimmed
away from both sides of the rib bone to a depth of
approximately 1½ inches. They are usually served with
paper frills on the bone.*

SCOTCH CHOPS *are sliced from the Scotch roast, which
is made from a whole lamb breast by slitting between*

breast bones and inner skin to form a pocket into which ground lamb is stuffed. The resulting Scotch roast can then be chilled and sliced into Scotch chops for pan-frying or broiling.

SIRLOIN CHOPS *are from the sirloin section which forms the upper portion of the leg.*

BLADE-BONE SHOULDER CHOPS *are from the blade-bone side of the square-cut shoulder.*

ROUND-BONE SHOULDER CHOPS *are from the arm-bone side of the square-cut shoulder.*

English Lamb Chops with Curry Sauce

Makes 4 servings

2 tablespoons butter	¼ teaspoon pepper
1 large onion, sliced	2 cups stock or bouillon
1½ cups chopped apples	1 tablespoon lemon juice
¼ cup all-purpose flour	½ cup flaked coconut
2 tablespoons curry powder	4 English lamb chops, about ¾ inch thick
1 teaspoon salt	

Melt butter; add onion and apples and cook 5 minutes over low heat, stirring occasionally. Add flour, curry powder, salt, and pepper; blend. Gradually add stock or bouillon and lemon juice. Cook over low heat, stirring constantly, until slightly thickened. Cover and cook 20 minutes over low heat, stirring frequently. Add coconut; mix well.

Meanwhile, broil lamb chops, 3 to 4 inches from source of heat, 5 to 7 minutes. Turn and broil 5 to 7 minutes or until desired degree of doneness. Serve lamb chops with curry sauce.

❀

Walnut-Glazed Lamb Chops

Makes 2 to 4 servings

4 loin lamb chops, cut as
    thick as desired
Salt to taste

¼ cup honey
¼ cup ground walnuts

Broil chops, 3 to 4 inches from source of heat, 5 to 7 minutes. Salt, turn, and cook 5 to 7 minutes or to desired degree of doneness. Salt.

Meanwhile, combine honey and walnuts; top lamb with mixture. Broil 2 to 3 minutes longer.

❀

Lamb Chops & Tomato Broil

Makes 2 to 4 servings

4 loin lamb chops, about
    1 inch thick
1 tablespoon grated onion
1 teaspoon garlic salt

1 teaspoon salt
⅛ teaspoon pepper
2 medium-sized tomatoes,
    cut in half

Broil chops, 3 to 4 inches from source of heat; 6 to 7 minutes or until browned. Turn. Combine onion and seasonings; mix well. Arrange tomatoes on broiler rack with chops. Sprinkle chops and tomatoes with onion mixture. Broil 5 to 6 minutes or until chops are done.

❀

Corn & Lamb Outdoor Grill

Makes 2 to 4 servings

¼ cup melted butter	2 tablespoons vinegar
⅓ cup chili sauce	4 ears corn
2 tablespoons brown sugar	4 loin lamb chops, about 1 inch thick

Combine butter, chili sauce, sugar, and vinegar. Mix to blend. Brush corn with some of chili-sauce mixture. Wrap corn in heavy-duty aluminum foil. Broil, 3 to 4 inches from source of heat, or cook on outdoor grill, turning occasionally, for 1 hour or until done. Ten minutes before corn is done, brush lamb with some of chili-sauce mixture. Broil lamb, 3 to 4 inches from source of heat, or cook on outdoor grill 5 to 7 minutes on each side or until desired degree of doneness. Brush lamb frequently with remaining chili-sauce mixture during cooking time. Serve lamb with corn.

❈

Montevideo Lamb Chops

Makes 2 to 4 servings

3 tablespoons butter	2 tablespoons sugar
4 loin lamb chops, about 1 inch thick	2 tablespoons coffee
2 tablespoons prepared horseradish	2 egg yolks
	4 teaspoons grated Parmesan cheese

Melt butter; add lamb chops and cook over medium heat until browned on both sides. Remove lamb; reserve drippings. Add horseradish; mix with drippings in skillet. Arrange lamb in greased shallow casserole.

Combine sugar, coffee, and egg yolks; mix well. Cook over boiling water, stirring constantly, until thickened. Combine coffee sauce and horseradish mixture in skillet; mix well. Pour coffee mixture over lamb. Top with Parmesan cheese. Bake in oven at 350° for 30 minutes.

❊

Spanish Basque Lamb Rib Chops

Makes 6 servings

- 2 tablespoons butter
- 2 tablespoons olive oil
- 6 rib lamb chops, cut 1¼ to 1½ inches thick
- ¼ pound cooked ham, cut into ½-inch cubes
- 12 thinly cut pepperoni sausage slices (or sweet Italian sausage)
- 1 cup finely chopped onion
- 1 can (16 ounces) peeled tomatoes
- ½ teaspoon salt
- ⅛ teaspoon pepper

Set control dial on electric frying pan at 350° and preheat. Add butter and olive oil. Brown chops on both sides. Remove lamb chops from pan and set aside. Reduce heat control to 250°. Pour off drippings and reserve them. In the same pan, add 2 tablespoons reserved drippings, the cubed ham, sausage, and chopped onion. Cook until onion is golden brown. Chop tomatoes and add to meat-onion mixture. Bring to a boil; add salt and pepper. Place browned chops in the meat-onion mixture, making sure that all chops are well covered with the sauce. Cover tightly and cook slowly 20 minutes or until chops are done.

❊

Mexican Lamb Chops

Makes 2 to 4 servings

4 lamb rib chops, about
  1 inch thick
Salt and pepper to taste
1 can (12 ounces) whole-
  kernel corn
Water

1 chicken bouillon cube
1 clove garlic, crushed
½ cup sliced green pepper
¼ cup diced canned
  pimientos

Broil lamb chops, 3 to 4 inches from source of heat, 5 to
7 minutes on each side or to desired degree of doneness.
Salt and pepper as you turn the chops.

Meanwhile, drain corn; reserve liquid. Add enough water
to corn liquid to make 1 cup liquid. Combine corn liquid,
bouillon cube, and garlic and heat to boiling. Add corn,
green pepper, and pimientos. Cover and cook 5 to 10
minutes or until green pepper is tender. Serve with lamb.

❁

Lamb Rib Chops with Anchovies

Makes 2 to 4 servings

¼ cup olive or salad oil
¾ teaspoon salt
¾ teaspoon pepper
1 teaspoon oregano
1 clove garlic, chopped

4 rib lamb chops, about
  1 inch thick
4 anchovies, chopped
2 teaspoons lemon juice
2 teaspoons dry mustard

Combine oil, ½ teaspoon salt, ½ teaspoon pepper, ½
teaspoon oregano, and ½ clove garlic. Add chops. Chill
1 hour. Turn chops occasionally. Combine remaining ¼
teaspoon salt, ¼ teaspoon pepper, ½ teaspoon oregano,
½ clove garlic, anchovies, lemon juice, and mustard;
spread on chops. Broil, 3 to 4 inches from source of heat,

5 to 7 minutes. Turn chops. Spread with remaining anchovy mixture. Broil 5 to 7 minutes or to desired degree of doneness.

❁

Hawaiian Luau Lamb Chops

Makes 6 servings

6 pocketed lamb loin chops, 1½ inches thick
¾ teaspoon salt
½ teaspoon crushed marjoram
1 cup packaged bread stuffing
1 can (9 ounces) crushed pineapple
¼ cup golden raisins
¼ teaspoon dry mustard
¾ teaspoon ginger
2 tablespoons butter
1½ tablespoons grated orange peel
½ cup orange juice
1½ teaspoons cornstarch
1 stick cinnamon (1½ inches long)
¼ cup water
¼ cup curaçao or orange juice

Sprinkle lamb chops with ½ teaspoon of the salt and marjoram. Combine bread stuffing, undrained pineapple, raisins, mustard, and ½ teaspoon of the ginger. Mix well and stuff each chop lightly; wrap any remaining dressing in foil to bake along with chops. Brown chops well on both sides in butter in ovenproof skillet. Stir in orange peel and juice; cover. Bake chops and dressing in oven at 350° for 1 hour or until meat is fork-tender. In saucepan, mix together cornstarch, remaining ¼ teaspoon salt and ¼ teaspoon ginger, cinnamon, and water. Drain liquid from lamb chops and stir into cornstarch mixture; cook and stir over low heat until thickened and clear. Add curaçao or orange juice, and pour over chops. Garnish with orange slices, if desired.

❁

Parmesan Rib Chops

Makes 6 servings

1 clove garlic, minced
1 tablespoon olive or
   salad oil
3 tablespoons freshly
   grated Parmesan cheese
1/3 cup tomato sauce

1 tablespoon chopped
   parsley
Dash oregano
Dash freshly ground pepper
6 rib lamb chops, about
   3/4 inch thick

In small skillet, sauté garlic in oil; stir in cheese, tomato sauce, parsley, oregano, and pepper. Spread thin layer over top side of chops. Broil, 3 to 4 inches from source of heat, 5 to 7 minutes; turn and brush second side; broil chops 5 minutes longer or until desired degree of doneness.

❁

Lamb Skillet, Spanish Style

Makes 3 to 6 servings

6 rib lamb chops, about
   1 inch thick
1 1/2 cups sliced cooked
   potatoes
1 can (8 ounces) small
   white onions, drained
2 medium-sized carrots,

cut in 2-inch strips and
   cooked
1/3 cup sliced pimiento-
   stuffed olives
1 can (8 ounces) tomato
   sauce
1/2 teaspoon onion salt

Cook chops over low heat until browned on both sides. Add remaining ingredients. Cover and cook over low heat 30 minutes or until chops are tender.

❁

Indoor-Outdoor Lamb Skillet

Makes 2 to 4 servings

2 tablespoons butter
4 rib lamb chops, about
    1 inch thick
4 cups sliced yellow
    summer squash

½ cup sliced scallions
1 medium-sized tomato,
    cut in wedges
½ cup stock or bouillon

Melt butter in skillet; add lamb and cook until browned
on both sides. Drain off drippings if necessary. Add squash,
scallions, tomato, and stock or bouillon. Cover and cook
5 to 10 minutes or until vegetables are tender.

❁

Old-Fashioned Pot Pie

Makes 2 to 4 servings

2 packages quick-frozen
    whipped potatoes
1 package (10 ounces)
    frozen Brussels sprouts
3 tablespoons chopped
    chives
1 teaspoon salt

¼ teaspoon pepper
¼ cup chopped canned
    pimientos
¼ cup melted butter
4 rib lamb chops, 1 inch
    thick
Salt and pepper

Prepare potatoes following package directions. Cook
Brussels sprouts according to package directions. Drain
if necessary. Combine potatoes, Brussels sprouts, chives,
1 teaspoon salt, ¼ teaspoon pepper, pimientos, and butter;
mix. Turn into shallow baking dish. Top with lamb.
Sprinkle lamb with salt and pepper. Bake in oven at 350°
for 30 minutes.

❁

Tropical Lamb Steaks

Makes 4 servings

2 lamb leg steaks, about
¾ inch thick
Salt and pepper
1 can (1 pound) tomatoes

1 can flaked coconut
¼ cup vinegar
2 tablespoons sugar
½ teaspoon oregano

Broil steaks, 3 to 4 inches from source of heat, 10 minutes. Sprinkle with salt and pepper; turn. Combine remaining ingredients. Pour over lamb. Broil 10 minutes or to desired degree of doneness.

❈

Spicy Lamb Steaks

Makes 4 servings

2 tablespoons salad oil
1 tablespoon vinegar
2 teaspoons
Worcestershire sauce
1 clove garlic, crushed

1 teaspoon salt
¼ teaspoon pepper
½ teaspoon celery seed
2 lamb leg steaks, about
1 inch thick

Combine oil, vinegar, Worcestershire sauce, garlic, salt, pepper, and celery seed; mix well. Add lamb and chill 2 to 3 hours, turning lamb occasionally. Broil, 3 to 4 inches from source of heat, or cook on outdoor grill 7 to 10 minutes. Turn lamb and cook 7 to 10 minutes or until lamb is desired degree of doneness.

❈

Chutney-Barbecued Lamb Leg Steaks

Makes 4 servings

½ cup chopped chutney
1 tablespoon lemon juice
1 teaspoon curry powder
½ teaspoon ginger

¼ cup butter
2 lamb leg steaks, 1 inch thick

Combine chutney, lemon juice, curry powder, ginger, and butter. Cook 15 minutes over low heat, stirring occasionally. Brush lamb with chutney mixture. Broil, 3 to 4 inches from source of heat, or cook on outdoor grill 7 to 10 minutes on each side or until lamb is desired degree of doneness. Brush lamb frequently with chutney mixture during cooking period.

❀

Baked Orange Lamb Steaks

Makes 4 servings

2 lamb leg steaks, about ½ inch thick
1 teaspoon salt
2 medium-sized oranges, sliced
2 tablespoons brown sugar

½ teaspoon ginger
¼ teaspoon cloves
1 teaspoon dehydrated mint flakes
¼ cup melted butter

Arrange lamb in shallow baking dish. Sprinkle lamb with salt. Top lamb with oranges. Combine remaining ingredients; mix well. Pour over lamb and oranges. Bake in oven at 325° for 40 minutes or to desired degree of doneness.

❀

Lamb Steaks with Apple Rings

Makes 4 servings

2 lamb leg steaks, about
¾ inch thick
Salt and pepper
2 tablespoons sugar
2 tablespoons lemon juice

2 tablespoons butter or
margarine
2 medium-sized apples,
cored and sliced

Arrange lamb steaks in shallow baking dish. Sprinkle with salt and pepper. Bake in moderate (350°) oven 20 minutes. Combine sugar, lemon juice, and butter or margarine. Cook over low heat until butter or margarine melts. Arrange apple rings around steaks and brush with lemon glaze. Bake 20 minutes or until apple rings are tender. Garnish as desired.

❄

Lamb Steaks Teriyaki

Makes 2 servings

½ cup soy sauce
1 tablespoon brown sugar
¼ teaspoon ginger
¼ teaspoon nutmeg

2 tablespoons lemon juice
2 sirloin lamb steaks, 1½
inches thick

Combine soy sauce, brown sugar, ginger, nutmeg, and lemon juice. Pour over lamb steaks; refrigerate 3 hours or overnight. Broil steaks, 3 to 4 inches from heat, 5 to 6 minutes on each side or to desired degree of doneness; baste frequently with marinade.

❄

Stuffed Lamb Rib Chops Dijonnais

Makes 6 servings

6 double rib lamb chops,
about 2 inches thick
1 can (3 ounces) sliced
mushrooms
½ teaspoon salt

3 tablespoons dry sherry
1 egg, beaten
½ cup fine dry bread
crumbs
Salt and pepper

Using sharp knife, make slit from bone side between rib bones into center of meat on each chop. Drain mushrooms, reserving 2 tablespoons liquid. Mix together reserved mushroom liquid, ½ teaspoon salt, sherry, egg, mushrooms, and bread crumbs; stuff chops with mushroom mixture. Broil chops, 4 to 5 inches from source of heat, 12 minutes on each side or until desired degree of doneness, salting and sprinkling with pepper before turning.

NOTE: If desired, have the butcher French the chops. Before serving, place a paper frill on each chop.

❁

Chutney Sirloin Lamb Steaks

Makes 4 servings

4 sirloin lamb steaks, about
½ inch thick
Salt and pepper

½ cup chutney
8 thin slices lemon

Sprinkle lamb with salt and pepper. Broil, 3 to 4 inches from source of heat, 5 to 7 minutes. Turn; top with chutney and lemon slices. Broil 5 to 7 minutes or to desired degree of doneness.

❁

Lamb Rib Chops Continental

Makes 6 servings

6 double rib lamb chops, about 2 inches thick

2 tablespoons seedless raisins

½ teaspoon ginger

¼ teaspoon powdered cloves

2 tablespoons maple-blended syrup

2 tablespoons slivered blanched almonds

½ cup chopped dried apricots

Salt and pepper

Using a small sharp knife, make slit between rib bones into center of meat on each chop. Mix raisins, ginger, cloves, syrup, almonds, and apricots. Stuff each chop with apricot mixture. Broil chops, 3 to 4 inches from source of heat, or cook on outdoor grill 12 minutes on each side or to desired degree of doneness. Sprinkle with salt just before turning and again on other side before removing from broiler.

❀

Saratoga Lamb Chop Skillet

Makes 4 servings

2 tablespoons olive oil

4 Saratoga lamb chops, about ¾ inch thick

1 can (1 pound) peas

2 cups diced turnips

1 large onion, sliced

¼ cup chopped parsley

1 teaspoon salt

¼ teaspoon pepper

Parsley

Heat oil; add lamb chops and cook over medium heat until browned on both sides. Drain peas; reserve liquid. Add liquid from peas, turnips, onion, chopped parsley, salt, and pepper to lamb chops. Cover and cook over low heat about 40 minutes or until lamb chops are tender. Add peas and heat through. Garnish with parsley.

❊

Outdoor Lamb-Vegetable Skillet

Makes 4 servings

2 tablespoons Italian-style dressing
4 lamb shoulder chops, ¾ inch thick
1 can (9 ounces) pineapple tidbits
1 can (1 pound) onions
½ teaspoon basil
1 teaspoon salt
1 medium-sized green pepper, sliced
1 tablespoon all-purpose flour

Heat dressing in skillet; add lamb and cook until browned on both sides. Drain pineapple; reserve syrup. Drain onions; reserve liquid. Combine pineapple syrup, onion liquid, basil, and salt. Add to lamb. Cover and cook over low heat, turning occasionally, for 45 to 60 minutes or until desired degree of doneness. Add onions, green pepper, and pineapple to lamb. Cover and cook 10 minutes or until green pepper is tender. Slowly stir some of onion-liquid mixture into flour; stir this into remaining onion-liquid mixture in skillet. Cook over low heat, stirring constantly until thickened.

❊

Lamb Shoulder Steaks with Vegetables

Makes 4 servings

1 tablespoon butter
1 cup chopped chives
4 lamb shoulder steaks, about ¾ inch thick
1 teaspoon salt
¼ teaspoon pepper

1 teaspoon rosemary
¾ cup water
2 cups diced potatoes
2 cups sliced turnips
1 cup sliced celery

Melt butter in skillet; add chives and lamb and cook until lamb is browned on both sides. Add seasonings, rosemary, and water. Cook, covered, for 1 hour. Add remaining ingredients and cook 30 minutes, stirring occasionally.

❁

Sweet-and-Sour Lamb Chops

Makes 4 servings

4 shoulder lamb chops
1 tablespoon butter
¼ cup vinegar
¼ cup firmly packed brown sugar
1 teaspoon salt

⅛ teaspoon pepper
¼ teaspoon ginger
1 medium-sized orange, sliced
1 medium-sized lemon, cut in wedges

Melt butter; add lamb and cook over low heat until browned on both sides. Drain. Combine vinegar, sugar, salt, pepper, and ginger; mix well. Pour over chops. Add remaining ingredients. Cover and cook over low heat about 20 minutes or until chops are tender.

❁

Lamb Chops Orientale

Makes 6 servings

6 loin lamb chops, 1 inch thick
Salt and pepper

1 can (1 pound) chicken chow mein
Hot cooked rice

Place lamb chops in skillet. Cook slowly, turning occasionally until brown. Season with salt and pepper. Add chow mein; heat thoroughly. Serve with rice.

❖

Broiled Loin Lamb Chops with Barbecue Sauce

Makes 2 to 4 servings

4 loin lamb chops, about 1 inch thick
Salt and pepper to taste
⅓ cup catsup

¼ cup chili sauce
¼ cup firmly packed brown sugar
4 slices onion

Broil lamb chops, 3 to 4 inches from source of heat, 6 to 7 minutes. Sprinkle with salt and pepper. Turn and broil 5 minutes.

Meanwhile, combine catsup, chili sauce, and sugar; mix well. Top chops with onion and catsup mixture. Broil 2 to 3 minutes or to desired degree of doneness.

❖

Lamb Chop & Fruit Skillet

Makes 4 servings

2 tablespoons butter
4 shoulder lamb chops, about ¾ inch thick
1 can (14 ounces) pineapple chunks
1 tablespoon cornstarch

2 tablespoons water
½ cup sliced peaches (fresh or canned)
1 medium-sized banana, sliced

Melt butter; add lamb and cook over low heat until browned on both sides. Add undrained pineapple chunks; cover and cook 25 minutes. Combine cornstarch and water; blend. Remove lamb chops. Add cornstarch mixture to pineapple mixture; mix well. Cook over low heat, stirring constantly, until thickened. Add lamb, peaches, and banana. Cover and cook 5 minutes. Serve with rice, as desired.

❋

Lamb & Cabbage

Makes 4 servings

4 lamb shoulder steaks, about ¾ inch thick
1 clove garlic, finely chopped
¼ teaspoon rosemary

⅔ cup cider vinegar
⅔ cup water
½ teaspoon salt
1 small head cabbage, cut in wedges

Place lamb in skillet. Combine garlic, rosemary, vinegar, water, and salt. Add to lamb; cover and cook over low heat 1 hour or until tender. Add cabbage; cover and cook 20 minutes.

❋

Lamb Shoulder Chops with Cranberry Stuffing

Makes 6 servings

½ cup butter
1 cup water
1 package (8 ounces) bread-stuffing mix
2 medium-sized oranges, chopped
2 cups cranberries
½ cup walnuts
6 lamb shoulder chops, about ¾ inch thick
Salt

Combine butter and water. Heat to boiling point. Add stuffing mix, oranges, cranberries, and walnuts; mix well. Turn into greased 2-quart shallow baking dish. Top with lamb. Sprinkle lamb with salt. Bake in oven at 350° for 30 minutes or until lamb is desired degree of doneness.

❖

Scotch Chops with Zesty Mint Sauce

Makes 4 servings

4 Scotch lamb chops, about 1 inch thick
Salt and pepper
½ cup bottled mint sauce
⅓ cup orange juice
¼ cup sugar
1 tablespoon cornstarch

Sprinkle lamb chops with salt and pepper. Broil 3 to 4 inches from source of heat, or cook on outdoor grill 5 to 7 minutes. Turn and cook 5 to 7 minutes or until desired degree of doneness.

Meanwhile, combine mint sauce, orange juice, and sugar; mix well. Add cornstarch; blend. Cook over low heat, stirring constantly, until thickened and clear. Serve mint sauce with lamb chops.

❖

Chinese Lamb Skillet I

Makes 4 servings

2 tablespoons salad oil
4 shoulder lamb chops, about ¾ inch thick
1 medium-sized onion, sliced
⅓ cup diced green pepper
⅓ cup diced celery
1 can (5 ounces) sliced bamboo shoots
1 can (1 pound) bean sprouts
½ teaspoon salt
¼ teaspoon pepper
1 tablespoon cornstarch
1½ teaspoons soy sauce
1 tablespoon water
1 medium-sized tomato, cut in wedges

Heat oil; add lamb, onion, green pepper, and celery. Cook until lamb is browned on both sides. Drain bamboo shoots and bean sprouts; reserve liquids and add them to lamb. Cover and cook lamb 30 minutes or until tender. Add bamboo shoots and bean sprouts to lamb mixture. Combine salt, pepper, and cornstarch; stir in soy sauce and water. Stir cornstarch mixture into lamb mixture; add tomato wedges. Cover and cook 5 minutes or until sauce thickens.

❖

Chinese Lamb Skillet II

Makes 6 servings

2 tablespoons salad oil
2 thin slices onion
¼ teaspoon ginger
6 shoulder lamb chops, 1 inch thick
1 can (5 ounces) water chestnuts
1 can (10¾ ounces) condensed cream of vegetable soup
1½ teaspoons soy sauce
⅔ cup sliced celery
Hot cooked rice

Heat oil in skillet; add onion slices, ginger, and lamb chops and cook until chops are browned on both sides. Drain off drippings. Measure liquid from water chestnuts; add water to make ¾ cup. Stir into skillet with undiluted soup and soy sauce. Slice chestnuts and add to skillet with celery. Cover and simmer 45 minutes or until lamb is tender. Serve over rice.

❊

Chinese Chops

Makes 4 servings

½ cup soy sauce
3 tablespoons olive oil
2 tablespoons lemon juice
1 tablespoon vinegar
1 large onion, grated
1 tablespoon sugar

¼ teaspoon pepper
1 clove garlic, crushed
1 bay leaf
Pinch oregano
4 shoulder lamb chops, about ½ inch thick

Combine soy sauce, olive oil, lemon juice, vinegar, onion, sugar, pepper, garlic, bay leaf, and oregano. Pour over shoulder chops and chill at least 2 hours, turning occasionally. Place chops and soy-sauce mixture in skillet; cover and simmer about 45 minutes or until tender. Serve with rice or noodles, if desired.

❊

Swedish Braised Lamb Chops

Makes 6 servings

6 shoulder lamb chops,
1 inch thick
1 teaspoon salt
1/2 teaspoon pepper
2 tablespoons butter
1 cup water
1 medium-sized onion,
sliced
2 bay leaves
1/2 teaspoon whole allspice
1/4 cup water
2 tablespoons flour
1/3 cup commercial sour
cream
1 teaspoon sugar

Sprinkle lamb with salt and pepper. Brown on both sides in butter in skillet; drain off drippings. Add 1 cup water, onion, bay leaves, and allspice; simmer 1 1/2 hours or until meat is fork-tender. Remove lamb. Mix 1/4 cup water with flour and stir into skillet. Blend in sour cream and sugar. Return lamb to sauce and heat through.

❁

Breezoles Stin Skara
(Broiled Lamb Chops)

Makes 4 to 8 servings

8 loin lamb chops, 1 inch
thick
1/4 cup butter
Juice of 1/2 lemon
1 teaspoon salt
1/4 teaspoon pepper
1 teaspoon oregano

Place chops on medium rack of broiler or grill. In a small saucepan, melt butter and add other ingredients. When chops begin to sizzle, brush generously with butter mixture. Turn after 5 to 6 minutes and brush other side generously.

Continue cooking until done (12 to 15 minutes in all for average chops). If more butter remains, brush again before last few minutes of cooking.

❋

Dill Shoulder Chops Continental

Makes 6 servings

2 tablespoons salad oil
6 shoulder lamb chops, about ¾ inch thick
Seasoned salt
1 vegetable-bouillon cube
1 cup boiling water
½ cup sliced celery
½ cup diced green pepper
1 can (3 ounces) sliced mushrooms
3 tablespoons flour
1 tablespoon chili sauce
2 teaspoons chopped fresh dill
½ cup commercial sour cream

Heat oil in large skillet; add lamb and sprinkle with seasoned salt. Brown on both sides; drain off drippings. Dissolve bouillon cube in boiling water, add to lamb with celery and green pepper. Cover and cook over low heat 30 minutes or until lamb is tender. Remove lamb from skillet. Drain mushrooms, and blend liquid into flour. Add to skillet with chili sauce and cook, stirring constantly, until sauce thickens. Add lamb, mushrooms, and dill. Top each chop with a spoonful of sour cream; cover and cook 5 minutes longer.

❋

Peruvian Shoulder Chops & Scallions

Makes 4 servings

3 tablespoons all-purpose flour

1 teaspoon salt

¼ teaspoon pepper

½ teaspoon oregano

4 lamb shoulder chops, about ¾ inch thick

¼ cup salad oil

¼ cup chopped scallions

¼ cup coffee

¼ cup commercial sour cream

¼ cup (about 1 ounce) grated Gruyère cheese

Combine flour, salt and pepper, and oregano; mix well. Pound flour mixture into lamb. Heat oil; add lamb and scallions and cook over medium heat until lamb is browned on both sides. Arrange lamb and scallions in a greased shallow casserole. Combine coffee and sour cream; mix well. Pour sour cream mixture over lamb. Top with cheese. Bake in oven at 350° for 30 minutes.

❁

Lamb Chops Romano

Makes 6 servings

6 shoulder lamb chops, about 1 inch thick

1 envelope (⅝ ounce) Italian salad-dressing mix

⅔ cup salad oil

¼ cup lemon juice

¼ cup water

1 teaspoon oregano

1 teaspoon sugar

Arrange lamb in shallow baking dish. Combine and mix together remaining ingredients; pour over lamb. Chill several hours, turning occasionally. Broil, 4 inches from source of heat, 10 to 15 minutes, brushing occasionally with marinade. Turn; cook about 10 minutes longer or until desired degree of doneness, brushing with marinade as needed.

❄

Scotch Lamb Chops with Fruit

Makes 4 servings

4 Scotch lamb chops, about 1 inch thick
½ cup chopped celery
1 can (1 pound, 4 ounces) sliced pineapple°
2 tablespoons orange juice
⅓ cup chopped mint
¼ cup chopped parsley
1 tablespoon grated orange rind
Salt and pepper to taste

Cook chops and celery in skillet over low heat until chops are browned on both sides. Drain off drippings. Drain pineapple; reserve ¼ cup syrup. Add ¼ cup pineapple syrup, orange juice, mint, parsley, orange rind, and salt and pepper to lamb mixture. Top with pineapple slices. Cover and cook over low heat about 45 minutes or until chops are done.

N O T E : If desired, ⅛ teaspoon cloves may be added with orange-juice mixture.

° One medium-sized pineapple, pared, cored, and sliced, may be substituted. In that case use 6 tablespoons orange juice.

❄

Lamb Chops With Rice

Makes 4 servings

- 1 tablespoon salad oil
- 4 shoulder lamb chops, ¾ inch thick
- 2 medium-sized onions, sliced
- 1 cup chopped celery
- 2 tablespoons all-purpose flour
- 1 cup stock or bouillon
- ¼ cup chopped canned pimiento
- 1 small clove garlic, crushed
- ½ teaspoon thyme
- 1 teaspoon salt
- ⅛ teaspoon pepper
- 2 tablespoons chopped parsley
- Cooked rice

Heat salad oil; add lamb chops, onions, and celery. Cook over medium heat until lamb is browned on both sides. Add flour; blend. Add stock or bouillon, stirring constantly. Add pimientos, garlic, thyme, salt, pepper, and parsley; mix well. Cover and cook over medium heat, stirring occasionally, 20 minutes or until lamb is done. Serve with rice.

❈

Lamb Chops Madrid

Makes 6 servings

- 6 shoulder lamb chops, about ¾ inch thick
- 2 tablespoons butter
- ½ teaspoon salt
- ¼ teaspoon pepper
- 1 package (2¼ ounces) spaghetti-sauce mix with mushrooms
- 1½ cups water
- 1 medium-sized onion, sliced
- 1 can (3 ounces) sliced mushrooms
- ½ cup ripe olives, sliced
- ¼ cup Marsala

In skillet, sauté lamb chops in butter over medium heat until browned. Sprinkle with salt and pepper. Stir together sauce mix and water; pour over lamb chops, cover and simmer 30 minutes, stirring occasionally. Stir in onion, undrained mushrooms, olives, and wine, and cook 15 minutes longer or until completely tender.

❋

Arabian Lamb Chops

Makes 4 servings

4 shoulder lamb chops, about 1 inch thick
1 tablespoon salad oil
Salt and pepper
2 tablespoons hot water
¼ cup mint jelly

1 medium-sized onion, sliced
1 medium-sized green pepper, chopped
2 medium-sized tomatoes, sliced
¼ teaspoon salt

Brown chops in hot oil in skillet. Drain off fat. Sprinkle with salt and pepper. Add hot water and mint jelly to lamb. Arrange onion slices and green pepper on top. Cover; simmer 30 minutes. Arrange tomato slices over all; sprinkle with ¼ teaspoon salt; cover and simmer 10 minutes longer or until lamb is tender.

❋

Lamb Chops in Wine Sauce

Makes 4 servings

- 2 tablespoons salad oil
- 1 medium-sized onion, chopped
- 1 clove garlic, chopped
- 4 shoulder lamb chops, about ¾ inch thick
- ½ teaspoon salt
- ¼ cup dry white wine
- ⅓ cup stock or bouillon
- 2 tablespoons tomato paste

Heat oil; add onion and garlic and cook 5 minutes over medium heat, stirring occasionally. Sprinkle lamb with salt. Add lamb to onion mixture and cook over medium heat until browned on both sides. Combine wine, stock or bouillon, and tomato paste; mix well. Pour over lamb mixture. Cover and cook 40 minutes over low heat, stirring occasionally. Serve lamb with sauce.

❀

Lamb Chop Skillet

Makes 4 servings

- 2 tablespoons butter
- 4 shoulder lamb chops, about ¾ inch thick
- ⅓ cup chopped celery
- 1 small onion, chopped
- ½ cup chopped green pepper
- 1 tablespoon chopped chives
- ½ cup water
- 1 beef-bouillon cube
- 2 medium-sized tomatoes, cut in wedges
- 2 teaspoons cornstarch
- 2 tablespoons water

Melt butter; add lamb and cook over low heat until browned on both sides. Add celery, onion, green pepper, and chives, and cook 5 minutes. Add ½ cup water and bouillon cube;

mix well. Cook, covered, over low heat 30 minutes. Add tomatoes and cook 5 minutes. Remove chops and tomatoes and arrange on platter. Mix cornstarch with water and combine with green-pepper mixture. Cook, stirring constantly, until thickened and clear. Serve with chops and tomatoes.

❀

Index